D1230138

U.S. v. Eichman:

FLAG BURNING AND FREE SPEECH

SUPREME COURT MILESTONES

U.S. v. Eichman:

FLAG BURNING AND FREE SPEECH

RON FRIDELL

Marshall Cavendish
Benchmark
New York

With special thanks to Professor David M. O'Brien of the Woodrow Wilson Department of Politics at the University of Virginia for reviewing the text of this book.

Marshall Cavendish Benchmark
99 White Plains Road
Tarrytown, NY 10591
www.marshallcavendish.us

Library of Congress Cataloging-in-Publication Data

Fridell, Ron.
    U.S. v. Eichman : flag burning and free speech / by Ron Fridell.
        p. cm. — (Supreme Court milestones)
    Includes bibliographical references and index.
    ISBN 978-0-7614-2953-1
    1. Eichman, Shawn (Shawn D.)—Trials, litigation, etc.   2. Johnson, Gregory Lee—Trials, litigation, etc.   3. Flags—Desecration—United States.
4. Flags—Law and legislation—United States—Criminal provisions.   5. Freedom of speech—United States.   I. Title.
KF224.E42F75 2008
342.7308'54—dc22
2007022595

Photo research by Connie Gardner

Cover photo by Charles Tasnadi/AP Photo

The photographs in this book are used by permission and through the courtesy of: *AP Photo*: 21, 29; Charles Tasnadi, 1; Marty Letterhandler, 80; Danny Johnston, 86; Jeff Markowitz, 102; *The Image Works*: David Lesson, 6; Mark Ludak, 49; *Corbis*: Bettmann, 10, 14, 34, 64, 69; UPI, 31; Seattle Post Intelligencer Collection/Museum of History and Industry, 40; Kevin Flemming, 42; Flip Shulke, 52; Wally McNamee, 63; Betsy Perdue, 82; Robert Maass, 119.

Publisher: Michelle Bisson
Art Director: Anahid Hamparian
Series Designer: Sonia Chaghatzbanian

Printed in: Malaysia
1 3 5 6 4 2

contents

Police take hold of Gregory Lee Johnson by the arms as they arrest him for flag desecration during the 1984 Republican National Convention.

one
FROM *JOHNSON* TO *EICHMAN*

SOMETIMES ONE U.S. SUPREME COURT case triggers another. *United States* v. *Eichman* (1990) was set in motion by *Texas* v. *Johnson* (1989). Both cases addressed the same question: Is it a criminal act to burn the U.S. flag as a protest against U.S. government policies?

Texas v. *Johnson* began when a Texas state trial court found Gregory Lee Johnson, a political protester, guilty of burning the U.S. flag, in violation of a state anti-flag-burning law. The case could have ended there, but Johnson appealed his trial court conviction to a state appeals court, and that began a series of appeals to higher and higher appeals courts.

A JUDICIAL MOUNTAIN

Moving through the U.S. appeals court system is like climbing a mountain. Along the way stands a series of appeals courts, also known as appellate courts, each one on a higher level than the last.

Each state has its own appeals court system, with a state supreme court and one or more appeals courts below it. Alongside these state appeals courts are federal appeals courts, which may review state cases that have passed through the state appeals courts, provided that a federal constitutional issue has been raised.

Appeals courts have a different purpose than trial

courts. They do not decide a defendant's guilt or innocence. Instead a panel of judges reviews the original trial
in order to rule on whether the decision was fair. Appeals
courts may also review lower appeals court rulings. The
judges ask: Were all parties treated fairly? Did they act
within the law? Were someone's constitutional rights violated, and if so, were the violations serious enough to war-
rant reversing the trial court verdict? At the top of this
judicial mountain stands the U.S. Supreme Court.

The first Texas state appeals court found the *Texas* v.
Johnson trial court's ruling unconstitutional, and that
appeals court reversed the guilty verdict. The state of Texas
then appealed that reversal to a higher-level appeals court,
which reinstated the trial court's original guilty verdict.
Johnson then appealed that reversal, and the case continued through the appeals system.

The case could have ended anywhere along the way, but
neither side would give in. *Texas* v. *Johnson* worked its way
up the judicial mountain all the way to the highest appeals
court in the land, the U.S. Supreme Court.

LAWMAKERS RESPOND

In its *Texas* v. *Johnson* decision, handed down in June 1989,
the Supreme Court ruled in favor of Johnson. It declared the
Texas law under which he was tried to be unconstitutional.
To protest government policies by burning the U.S. flag
was not a criminal offense, the Court ruled. It was a legal
act of free expression protected by the establishment
clause of the First Amendment of the Bill of Rights:

> Congress shall make no law respecting an estab-
> lishment of religion, or prohibiting the free exer-
> cise thereof; or abridging the freedom of speech,
> or of the press; or the right of the people peaceably
> to assemble, and to petition the Government for a

redress of grievances [compensation for harm suffered].

The U.S. Supreme Court's ruling in *Texas* v. *Johnson* was felt nationwide. In addition to Texas, forty-seven states had anti-flag-burning laws on the books. The Court's ruling made them all unconstitutional—null and void.

The *Texas* v. *Johnson* ruling outraged a great many members of Congress. Four months later they made a protest of their own by passing the Flag Protection Act of 1989 (FPA): "Whoever knowingly mutilates, defaces, physically defiles, burns, maintains on the floor or ground, or tramples upon any flag of the United States shall be fined under this title or imprisoned for not more than one year, or both."

THe seaTTLe proTesTers

The moment the FPA took effect, it caused exactly what it was meant to prevent. Citizens who saw the passage of the act as an attack on their constitutional right of free speech showed the government exactly how they felt. To protest the anti-flag-burning law, protesters began to burn flags.

The public demonstrations included protest rallies, with flag burnings in public places nationwide. Two of these demonstrations were destined to become part of U.S. Supreme Court history.

At midnight on October 28, 1989, in Seattle, Washington, a crowd estimated at five hundred gathered to demonstrate. Among the demonstrators was a small group who lowered a U.S. flag from its position atop a flagpole outside a post office, set it on fire, and ran it back up the pole. The group members had made their views known on leaflets that they handed out to the crowd:

> On October 28th it becomes illegal to desecrate the flag. This fascist law is not an "exception" to the

MANY PEOPLE WERE IN FAVOR OF THE CONSTITUTIONAL AMENDMENT THAT
FORBADE THE DESECRATION OF THE U.S. FLAG. THIS 1989 RALLY WAS STAGED
IN ITS SUPPORT.

concept of free speech but an attack on political protest and dissent, and a precedent for the future. Blind patriotism must not be the law of the land. Unlike the flag-kissers, we will not whine, we will Rock & Roll in a Festival of Defiance.

Four of the Seattle demonstrators were arrested. They were charged with knowingly burning a flag of the United States, in violation of the Flag Protection Act of 1989.

THE D.C. PROTESTERS

Two days later, in Washington, D.C., three other protesters burned a U.S. flag. They too made their views known in a leaflet:

> The battle lines are drawn. On one side stands the government and all those in favor of compulsory patriotism and enforced rever(e)nce to the flag. On the other side are all those opposed to this. And to all the oppressed we have this to say also. This flag means one thing to the powers that be and something else to all of us. Everything bad this system has done and continues to do to people all over the world has been done under this flag. No law, no amendment will change it, cover it up, or [stifle] that truth. So to you we say, Express yourself. Burn this flag. It's quick, it's easy, it may not be the law, but it's the right thing to do.

The police arrested the three protesters. Like the Seattle group, the D.C. protesters were charged with violating the FPA.

MOTIONS TO DISMISS

The protesters in both demonstrations were represented, free of charge, by attorneys from the Center for

Constitutional Rights. This organization refers to itself as "a non-profit legal and educational organization dedicated to protecting and advancing the rights guaranteed by the U.S. Constitution and the Universal Declaration of Human Rights."

In the months that followed, federal district courts in both Seattle and Washington, D.C., heard motions on behalf of the flag burners to have the charges dismissed. Both courts ruled in their favor, declaring that the Flag Protection Act of 1989 violated their First Amendment right of free speech.

The U.S. government appealed the district court rulings in both cases to the U.S. Supreme Court. The Court agreed to hear the two appeals and combined them into a single case, naming it *United States* v. *Eichman*, after Shawn Eichman, one of the Washington, D.C., flag burners. That made the United States the petitioner, or appellant, in the case. The flag burners were the respondents, or appellees.

TAKING SIDES

Members of the U.S. Congress made sure the Court knew which side they were on by filing *amicus curiae*, or friend of the court, briefs. A brief is a legal document that explains how the writer sees the legal issues involved in a case. Individuals or groups who are vitally interested in a case may file *amicus* briefs, arguing for the petitioner or respondent. Justices receive copies to read and may be influenced by the arguments they present. The House and Senate briefs, not surprisingly, were in support of the petitioner.

The *Eichman* case would focus on the Flag Protection Act of 1989. In their briefs, members of Congress argued that the new statute was not a violation of freedom of speech, since it made no mention of the protesters' right to express themselves through speaking or writing. The act was designed only to protect the flag itself from actions causing it physical harm, they argued.

The president himself joined in by making a public statement. George H. W. Bush declared himself in favor of protecting the flag and punishing those who would physically harm it. "Flag burning is wrong," he declared in no uncertain terms.

Free Speech Limits

So it would be up to the nine justices of the Supreme Court to provide answers to these questions: Should the federal government and the state governments be allowed to prosecute people who burn the U.S. flag in violation of the Flag Protection Act of 1989? Or does the act violate the First Amendment of the U.S. Constitution?

The case would be argued on May 14, 1990, and the ruling handed down a month later, on June 11. The decision would be close, with emotions running high on both sides. By the narrowest of margins, the Court would rule 5 to 4 in favor of the *Eichman* flag burners.

No U.S. Supreme Court ruling stands in isolation. Each decision is influenced by past rulings. All nine justices would take a thoughtful look back into legal history before deciding which way to vote on *United States* v. *Eichman*.

When justices review past U.S. Supreme Court rulings for guidance, they are looking at precedents. The precedent rulings the Court looked at concerned a variety of issues that had one thing in common: they all concerned the limits of freedom of speech. *United States* v. *Eichman* was, after all, a debate about free, or symbolic, speech.

YETTA STROMBERG WAS CONVICTED OF VIOLATING A CALIFORNIA LAW BECAUSE
SHE RAISED THE RED FLAG OF COMMUNISM EVERY DAY. THE SUPREME COURT
OVERTURNED HER CONVICTION ON THE GROUNDS OF FREEDOM OF SPEECH.

TWO
ARE ACTIONS SPEECH?

AN OLD PROVERB SAYS "Actions speak louder than words." But does that mean that actions themselves are a form of speech, just like speaking and writing? Here was a question that the justices in *Eichman* would have to consider: Is burning the U.S. flag a form of speech?

The same nine justices already had answered that question in *Texas* v. *Johnson*. Flag burning as a form of political protest was a form of speech protected by the First Amendment, they had ruled. But now, a year later, in *United States* v. *Eichman*, the U.S. government was asking the justices to reconsider their *Johnson* ruling and reverse it in light of the Flag Protection Act (FPA), the federal law under which the Seattle and the Washington, D.C., protesters had been arrested and tried.

The Texas state law under which Gregory Lee Johnson had been arrested and tried made it a crime to show contempt for the flag. But this new federal law under which the *Eichman* protesters had been arrested and tried treated flag burning as a purely physical act. Under the act, the petitioner argued, it didn't matter that the flag had been burned as a protest against U.S. government policies, as described in the protesters' leaflets. The respondents' political views and contempt for the flag were of no relevance. The only thing that mattered, as far as the government was concerned, was that the protesters had deliberately and physically harmed the U.S. flag. And it was for that deliberate physical harm only that the respondents had been prosecuted, the petitioner insisted.

Thus the justices would have to decide whether the FPA was constitutional—whether burning the flag could be seen as a purely physical act, apart from the messages that the *Eichman* flag burners intended their actions to express. If so, then perhaps flag burning was no longer a legal form of speech and could now be classed as a criminal act, unprotected by the First Amendment.

Free speech precedent: *Stromberg* v. *California*

To help them decide the actions-as-speech issue, the *Eichman* justices would review three U.S. Supreme Court rulings in previous cases dealing with actions as speech: *Stromberg* v. *California* (1931), *Tinker* v. *Des Moines* (1969), and *Schacht* v. *United States* (1970).

Would these precedent cases support the petitioner's case in *Eichman*? The government was claiming that, under the FPA, flag burning could be seen as a purely physical act apart from any expression intended by the flag burners. Or did these cases support the respondents' case? The *Eichman* flag burners were claiming that burning a U.S. flag in protest of U.S. government policies was still a form of symbolic, expressive speech protected by the First Amendment.

At the center of the first precedent case, *Stromberg* v. *California*, was Yetta Stromberg, a nineteen-year-old counselor at a children's summer camp. She was also a member of the Young Communist League (YCL). The YCL was dedicated to changing the United States from a capitalist society to a socialist society modeled after the Soviet Union.

Every morning Yetta Stromberg would raise a red flag,

the flag of Soviet Russia, and have the children salute it. Stromberg was charged with violating a California statute outlawing the display of any flag that represented opposition to the U.S. government.

SYMBOLIC EXPRESSION

A California court found Stromberg guilty. She protested that the state had violated her right to free speech under the Fourteenth Amendment. Why the Fourteenth Amendment instead of the First?

Ideally, rights guaranteed by the Constitution are federal rights, guaranteed to all citizens. But in practice, states sometimes passed laws that denied citizens their federal rights. The Fourteenth Amendment, ratified in 1868, was supposed to put an end to that practice. One part of the amendment prohibited individual states from denying citizens their constitutional rights, including the right to freedom of speech:

> No State shall make or enforce any law which shall abridge the privileges or immunities of citizens of the United States; nor shall any State deprive any person of life, liberty, or property, without due process of law; nor deny to any person within its jurisdiction the equal protection of the laws.

The Fourteenth Amendment helped, but it did not put a complete stop to the practice of denying citizens their constitutional rights. That was why Stromberg's case eventually reached the U.S. Supreme Court.

Supreme Court rulings are handed down in the form of opinions agreed to by the justices who voted with the majority. Usually one justice is given the job of writing the majority opinion for the Court. In this case, it was Chief Justice Charles Evans Hughes.

The Court ruled in favor of Yetta Stromberg. Her act of displaying the Soviet flag, Hughes wrote, was a symbolic expression of her opposition to the U.S. government. This symbolic act was protected by the First Amendment, just as any actual words Stromberg might have spoken or written in opposition to the government would have been. The California state court conviction of Stromberg was reversed.

THe importance of *stromberg*

Stromberg v. *California* was a landmark freedom-of-speech case. It was the first U.S. Supreme Court case in which the Court declared that nonverbal expression, including symbolic actions, could be protected as free speech, the same as spoken and written expression.

Though this case did not deal with flag burning specifically, it did establish a precedent to consider symbolic actions in general to be protected by the First Amendment. That made it an important ruling in support of the *Eichman* respondents.

Stromberg was important for another reason. Besides extending free speech, the majority opinion also spoke of limits:

> The right [of free speech] is not an absolute one. . . .
> There is no question but that the State may thus provide for the punishment of those who indulge in utterances which incite to violence and crime and threaten the overthrow of organized government by unlawful means. There is no constitutional immunity for such conduct abhorrent to our institutions.

That is, the states had a legitimate interest in maintaining order and were not barred from limiting speech that threatened that order. Here Hughes was addressing "special circumstances," exceptional situations where the majority ruling might not apply. As we will see, Hughes's cautious words would influence the Court to make exceptions to free speech protections in future cases.

In reviewing this precedent, the *Eichman* justices would be reminded that free speech was not an absolute right. There were instances in which the government could limit free speech protections for behavior that constituted "conduct abhorrent to our institutions." So while the *Stromberg* opinion supported the respondents' case, it also left open the possibility that "special circumstances" might some-how apply to the flag burners' actions in *Eichman*.

Free Speech Precedent: *Tinker* v. *Des Moines*

The *Stromberg* case focused on a Soviet flag. The *Tinker* case concerned black armbands. The full name of the case was *Tinker* v. *Des Moines Independent Community School District*.

The case was decided in 1969, during the long and highly unpopular Vietnam War (1959–1975). The Southeast Asian nation of Vietnam had been split in two, and the North was fighting the South in a bloody civil war. The North Vietnamese troops were supported by communist Chinese soldiers, while U.S. soldiers fought alongside the South Vietnamese troops.

The nationwide antiwar movement that had sprung up included students from universities, high schools, and even grade schools. These students called for U.S. troops to stop fighting in another nation's civil war and come home.

John Tinker, fifteen, and Christopher Eckhardt, sixteen, were high school students. Mary Beth Tinker, John Tinker's thirteen-year-old sister, attended junior high school. They were part of a group of seven students in the Des Moines, Iowa, schools who planned to protest the Vietnam War by wearing black armbands to class.

A Matter OF DISCIPLine

School officials learned of the students' plans and were waiting when they arrived. The students were given a choice: remove the armbands or face suspension. When the students refused to remove the armbands, they were suspended.

The parents of the Tinkers and of Christopher Eckhardt filed a lawsuit against the Des Moines schools, protesting the suspensions. The U.S. District Court in Des Moines dismissed their complaint. The reasons bring to mind Chief Justice Hughes's "special circumstances" concerns in the *Stromberg* v. *California* ruling. The District Court upheld the suspensions on the grounds that the armbands and the protest they symbolized would disturb school discipline.

After that decision was upheld by a U.S. Court of Appeals, the Supreme Court justices agreed to hear the case. The question before them was: Does a prohibition against the wearing of armbands in public schools, as a form of symbolic protest, violate the First Amendment's freedom of speech protections?

The U.S. Supreme Court ruling was handed down on February 24, 1969. By a 7 to 2 vote, the Court found in favor of the students. The majority opinion was written by Justice Abe Fortas. The wearing of armbands, he wrote, "was closely akin to 'pure speech' which, we have repeatedly held, is entitled to comprehensive protection under the First Amendment."

ArmBanDs anD SPecIaL cIrcumsTances

Like *Stromberg*, the *Tinker* opinion took care to point out special circumstances. Did students and teachers give up some of their constitutional rights to free speech when they were in the special environment of a school?

SUPREME COURT JUSTICE ABE FORTAS (FRONT) WROTE THE MAJORITY OPINION IN *Tinker* v. *Des Moines*, DECLARING THAT STUDENTS HAD AS MUCH RIGHT TO FREEDOM OF SPEECH AS ADULTS.

"Students in school as well as out of school are 'persons' under our Constitution," Fortas wrote. "They are possessed of fundamental rights which the State must respect, just as they themselves must respect their obligations to the State."

But what if their speech had caused a disturbance on the school campus? Fortas wrote:

In wearing armbands, the petitioners were quiet and passive. They were not disruptive and did not impinge upon the rights of others. In these circumstances, their conduct was within the protection of the Free Speech Clause of the First Amendment and the Due Process Clause of the Fourteenth.

The majority opinion is the one that decides the legal case. But justices who are in the minority generally write dissenting opinions explaining why they disagree. And those dissenting opinions may serve to influence future justices, such as those involved in the *Eichman* case. Justice Hugo Black strongly disagreed with the majority opinion. In his dissent, Justice Black wrote:

[I]f the time has come when pupils of state-supported schools, kindergartens, grammar schools, or high schools, can defy and flout orders of school officials to keep their minds on their own schoolwork, it is the beginning of a new revolutionary era of permissiveness in this country fostered by the judiciary.

The Vietnam era was a volatile period in which an unpopular war elicited passionate emotional reactions from adults and young people alike. This "new revolutionary era of permissiveness . . . fostered by the judiciary," as Justice Black saw it, meant that, thanks in part to the Court, students in schools could now feel free to express their political opinions directly.

To Justice Black this new standard of freedom was a distraction for students. It went too far in upholding freedom of speech. Justice Black's dissent brought up questions that the *Eichman* justices would have to consider: What are the limits of freedom of speech? Is the freedom to burn the flag too much freedom?

THe importance of *Tinker*

In his majority opinion, Fortas cited *Stromberg* as precedent. After the *Tinker* ruling, both flying a Soviet flag and wearing black armbands in protest of government policies were officially recognized as forms of legally protected speech. Though neither *Stromberg* nor *Tinker* mentioned flag burning, both precedents strengthened the legal principle that symbolic actions protesting government policy were protected by the First Amendment, a principle that supported the *Eichman* respondents' case.

Even though dissenting opinions do not have the authority of law, they can influence future decisions. Justice Black's vigorous dissent pointed to a need to be conservative in granting free speech rights, an attitude that recalled Hughes's cautions in the *Stromberg* opinion and an attitude that could be seen to help the petitioner's case in *Eichman*.

Free speech precedent: *SCHACHT* V. *UNITED STATES*

Like *Tinker*, *Schacht* v. *United States* (1970) grew out of an anti-Vietnam War protest. This one took the form of a skit, a short play, performed in front of an armed forces induction center in Houston, Texas.

One of the actors, Daniel Jay Schacht, wore a U.S. military uniform, though he himself was not a soldier.

U.S. supreme court profile

The Supreme Court is the highest court in the United States. Among its defining characteristics are the following:

- The Supreme Court was created by Article III, Sections 1 and 2, of the U.S. Constitution. The Court decided its first case in 1792.

- The Court meets regularly from early October to late June in the Supreme Court Building, located at 1 First Street, Washington, D.C.

- It has nine members, known as justices. One is the chief justice. The other eight are associate justices. All the justices are appointed for life by the president, with the advice and consent of the Senate.

- The Supreme Court is charged with ensuring that all citizens receive equal justice under the law and that the rights guaranteed to citizens by the Constitution are protected.

- Juries are not involved in Supreme Court cases. Instead, the Court reviews lower court decisions that raise conflicts between the Constitution and federal or state law. Its rulings are meant to preserve the Constitution.

- Once the Court makes a ruling, the other U.S. courts are expected to follow its decisions in similar cases.

Schacht was arrested and then convicted of violating a Texas law that said "Whoever, in any place within the jurisdiction of the United States . . . without authority, wears the uniform . . . of any of the armed forces of the United States . . . shall be fined under this title or imprisoned not more than six months, or both."

In appealing his conviction, Schacht claimed that he was, in fact, legally authorized to wear the uniform by an act of Congress. The act permits an actor to wear a military uniform in a play or motion picture production "if the portrayal does not tend to discredit that armed force."

A court of appeals rejected his appeal, so Schacht appealed to the U.S. Supreme Court. In his appeal, Schacht claimed that these words in the act of Congress— "if the portrayal does not tend to discredit that armed force"—made it unconstitutional, since the act unjustly restrained his freedom of speech.

uniforms and speech

The Court agreed to hear the case. The ruling was handed down in May 1970. The Court found in favor of Schacht. The majority opinion was written by Justice Hugo Black, the same justice who had written a dissenting opinion in the *Tinker* case a year earlier. Justice Black wrote:

> An actor, like everyone else in our country, enjoys a constitutional right to freedom of speech, including the right openly to criticize the Government during a dramatic performance. . . . [H]is conviction can be sustained only if he can be punished for speaking out against the role of our Army and our country in Vietnam. Clearly punishment for this reason would be an unconstitutional abridgment of freedom of speech.

THE IMPORTANCE OF *SCHACHT*

The free speech issue in *Stromberg* was displaying a foreign flag as a protest against government policies. In *Tinker* it concerned wearing an armband in protest of a war. With *Schacht* it was wearing a military uniform at a public performance in protest of the war.

All three rulings extended freedom of speech protections to symbolic actions. And all three extended those protections to people who were expressing their disagreement with U.S. government policies. So all three rulings could be said to support the respondents in *Eichman* and weaken the case for the petitioner.

But what about the cautions expressed by Hughes in *Stromberg* and by Black in *Tinker*? And what about precedent cases that put limits on the freedom of speech?

THREE
SETTING LIMITS:
THE O'BRIEN TEST

ANOTHER CASE THAT FOCUSED on free speech and symbolic action was *United States v. O'Brien* (1968). But unlike *Stromberg*, *Tinker*, and *Schacht*, the *O'Brien* precedent did not extend free speech rights to symbolic actions. It limited them. In *O'Brien* the justices delineated a set of conditions under which the government could limit freedom of speech in regard to symbolic actions such as those taken by the *Eichman* flag burners. This set of conditions became known as the O'Brien test, a standard that would figure prominently in the *Eichman* decision.

FREE SPEECH PRECEDENT: *UNITED STATES V. O'BRIEN*

On the morning of March 31, 1966, David Paul O'Brien and three friends gathered at the South Boston Courthouse. On the courthouse steps O'Brien and his friends publicly burned their Selective Service registration certificates, also known as draft cards.

These events took place during the Vietnam War, when a military draft was in effect. When a male reached the age of eighteen, he was required to register with a local draft board, which assigned him a Selective Service number and a classification. Some registrants received a classification

Draft Cards

The *O'Brien* majority opinion included this description of a draft card:

> Both the registration and classification certificates are small white cards, approximately 2 by 3 inches. The registration certificate specifies the name of the registrant, the date of registration, and the number and address of the local board with which he is registered. Also inscribed upon it are the date and place of the registrant's birth, his residence at registration, his physical description, his signature, and his Selective Service number. The Selective Service number itself indicates his State of registration, his local board, his year of birth, and his chronological position in the local board's classification record.

of 4-F, meaning they were physically or mentally unfit to serve in the armed forces. Others received deferments, or grace periods that delayed their being drafted so that they could, for instance, finish college study. Most males were classified 1-A, meaning they would have to enter the armed services to help fight the Vietnam War if they were asked.

A person's classification was shown on a draft card, which all males who were eligible for the draft were required to have in their possession. When David Paul O'Brien and his friends burned their draft cards, they broke a federal law that applies to any person "who forges, alters, knowingly destroys, knowingly mutilates, or in any manner changes any such certificate. . . ."

A MAN WEARING THE UNIFORM AND GREEN BERET OF THE U.S. SPECIAL FORCES HOLDS UP HIS DRAFT CARD BEFORE THROWING IT INTO A FIRE SET BY PROTESTERS AGAINST THE VIETNAM WAR IN NEW YORK'S CENTRAL PARK IN 1967.

Congress had passed this 1965 law, an amendment to the Universal Military Training and Service Act, in reaction to a series of anti-Vietnam War protests that included the burning of draft cards. Congress's reaction then was similar to the reaction it would have more than twenty years later, when another U.S. Congress passed the Flag

Protection Act of 1989 in reaction to the Supreme Court's ruling in *Texas* v. *Johnson*.

THE LOWER COURTS

A sizable crowd witnessed the burning. Among them were several agents of the Federal Bureau of Investigation (FBI). They took O'Brien inside the courthouse, where he stated that he had burned his draft card in hopes of influencing others in the crowd to adopt his antiwar beliefs.

O'Brien was arrested for violating the 1965 amendment to the Selective Service Act by burning his draft card. He was found guilty and then appealed. The U.S. Court of Appeals ruled that the 1965 amendment that made draft-card burning a crime was unconstitutional, since its intent was to punish people for criticizing the government. Therefore O'Brien's original conviction was reversed.

But the appeals court found that O'Brien was still guilty of the lesser crime of failing to have a draft card in his possession. The U.S. government then appealed that ruling, arguing that the appeals court was wrong to declare the 1965 amendment unconstitutional. The U.S. Supreme Court agreed to hear the government's appeal.

THE SUPREME COURT RULING

The Court handed down its ruling in *United States* v. *O'Brien* on May 27, 1968. Chief Justice Earl Warren wrote the majority opinion. By a vote of 7 to 1 (Thurgood Marshall did not vote), the Court ruled in favor of the government. "We hold that the 1965 Amendment is constitutional both as enacted and as applied. . . . A law prohibiting destruction of Selective Service certificates no more abridges free speech on its face than a motor vehicle law prohibiting the destruction of drivers' licenses, or a tax law prohibiting the destruction of books and records."

The opinion contrasts O'Brien's actions with Yetta

DAVID O'BRIEN BURNED HIS DRAFT CARD IN PROTEST AGAINST THE VIETNAM WAR. THE SUPREME COURT RULED AGAINST HIM. AT A PRESS CONFERENCE AFTER THE COURT VOTED 7 TO 1 IN FAVOR OF THE GOVERNMENT, O'BRIEN SAT WITH HIS WIFE, PAULA, AND SAID HE WAS "SHOCKED AT THE DECISION."

Stromberg's. The lower court found her guilty for her negative views of the U.S. government, and for those views only, Justice Warren wrote.

This was not the case with O'Brien. Although he too was expressing antigovernment views (speech), he was also destroying a document that he was required to have in his possession (nonspeech). "This Court has held that when 'speech' and 'nonspeech' elements are combined in the same course of conduct, a sufficiently important governmental interest in regulating the nonspeech element can justify incidental limitations on First Amendment freedoms."

THE FOUR IFS

In the majority opinion the justices set down a four-point test for dealing with speech and nonspeech elements when, as in O'Brien's draft-card burning, they occur together. It would become known as the O'Brien test.

[W]e think it clear that a government regulation is sufficiently justified (1) if it is within the constitutional power of the Government; (2) if it furthers an important or substantial governmental interest; (3) if the governmental interest is unrelated to the suppression of free expression; and (4) if the incidental restriction on alleged First Amendment freedoms is no greater than is essential to the furtherance of that interest.

In other words, a law that involves regulating expressive speech or action must meet these four standards: (1) It must be constitutional; (2) it must further an objective that is vitally important to the functioning of the government; (3) that vital objective cannot include the government's deliberate suppression of free speech; (4) if any suppression of free speech is involved, it must be incidental and narrowly drawn. In the *O'Brien* case, the Court found that:

> The governmental interest and the scope of the 1965 Amendment are limited to preventing harm to the smooth and efficient functioning of the Selective Service System. When O'Brien deliberately rendered unavailable his registration certificate, he willfully frustrated this governmental interest. For this noncommunicative impact of his conduct, and for nothing else, he was convicted. . . . [Therefore] [w]e find that the 1965 Amendment to . . . the Universal Military Training and Service Act meets all of these requirements, and consequently that O'Brien can be constitutionally convicted for violating it.

THE importance of *O'Brien*

In *O'Brien* the 1965 amendment to the Selective Service Act was put to the O'Brien test, and it passed. The justices ruled that protecting O'Brien's Selective Service card from physical harm was more important than protecting O'Brien's right of free speech to burn that card in protest of government policies.

In *Eichman*, the Flag Protection Act of 1989 was put to the O'Brien test. For the *Eichman* petitioners to win their case, they would have to convince the justices that protecting the U.S. flag from physical harm was more important than protecting the flag burners' right of free speech to burn the flag in protest of government policies.

OLIVER WENDELL HOLMES WROTE THE COURT'S UNANIMOUS OPINION IN
FAVOR OF THE U.S. GOVERNMENT IN THE *Schenck* CASE. HOLMES'S OPINION
SET LIMITS ON FREE SPEECH IN TIMES OF WAR.

four
SETTING LIMITS:
DANGEROUS WORDS

THE FOUR IFS are NOT THE ONLY legal standards set down in regard to limiting free speech. The *Eichman* justices would take into account two other tests in their decision: clear and present danger and fighting words.

In *Eichman* the petitioners and respondents would argue this question: Did the respondents' act of burning the U.S. flag to protest government policy constitute a threat to law and order serious enough that the government had both a right and duty to seek to prevent and punish that act? The following precedent cases would help the justices decide the answer.

FREE SPEECH PRECEDENT: *SCHENCK V. UNITED STATES*

During World War I (1914–1918), men were drafted into the U.S. armed forces to fight in Europe with the Allied Powers—led by France, Russia, the United Kingdom, and Italy—against the German Empire and the other Central Powers. It was a long and bloody war that ended with the defeat of the Central Powers.

Many U.S. citizens opposed the entry of the United States into the war, which occurred in 1917. Charles Schenck was among them. He mailed circulars to men who were likely to be drafted, suggesting that the draft was morally wrong and urging the men to resist being drafted and to protest the U.S. draft system by peaceful means.

Schenck was arrested and charged with conspiracy to violate the Espionage Act by attempting to obstruct military recruitment during a war. The Espionage Act had been passed in 1917 after the United States entered World War I to protect against obstruction of the military cause. Violators could go to jail for twenty years, be fined $100,000, and have additional penalties levied as well. A lower court convicted him, and Schenck appealed.

CLEAR AND PRESENT DANGER

The case eventually made its way to the U.S. Supreme Court. The question presented for the justices to decide was: Are Schenck's actions of distributing the leaflets protected by the free speech clause of the First Amendment?

The Court's majority opinion, handed down on March 3, 1919, was written by Justice Oliver Wendell Holmes. By a unanimous 9 to 0 vote, the Court found in favor of the U.S. government. Holmes wrote: "The question in every case is whether the words used are used in such circumstances and are of such a nature as to create a clear and present danger that they will bring about the substantive evils that Congress has a right to prevent."

The opinion agreed that, under normal circumstances, Schenck's activities might have been protected by the First Amendment. But in special circumstances such as wartime, speech can be restricted when it poses a "clear and present danger," that is, when speech poses a clear and present danger to public safety. To help define the term *clear and present danger*, Holmes wrote, "The most stringent protection of free speech would not protect a man in falsely shouting fire in a theatre and causing a panic."

The *Schenck* ruling does not directly parallel *Eichman*,

because Schenck's activities took place during wartime, while the *Eichman* protesters' actions did not. But, like *O'Brien*, the Schenck ruling does reinforce the legal principle that under certain special circumstances the government may limit a person's freedom of speech.

Free speech precedent: *Chaplinsky* v. *New Hampshire*

Besides the O'Brien test and the clear and present danger test, the *Eichman* justices would be considering the "fighting words" test, as outlined in the 1942 U.S. Supreme Court case *Chaplinsky* v. *New Hampshire*. It began one Saturday afternoon on a Rochester, New Hampshire, sidewalk.

Walter Chaplinsky, a Jehovah's Witness, distributed material about his religion to passersby. Citizens complained to the police that Chaplinsky was also loudly calling out that other religions were nothing but a racket. They said that Chaplinsky's angry words had started a small riot.

A police officer warned Chaplinsky to stop shouting. In response, Chaplinsky said, "You are a God damned racketeer" and "a damned Fascist and the whole government of Rochester are Fascists or agents of Fascists." (This incident occurred during World War II [1939–1945], while Adolf Hitler's fascist armies were overrunning Europe.)

FIGHTING WORDS

Chaplinsky was arrested and charged with violating a New Hampshire state statute that outlawed saying "any offensive, derisive or annoying word to any other person who is lawfully in any street or other public place," or calling him "by any offensive or derisive name."

In his defense Chaplinsky claimed that the statute was invalid under the Fourteenth Amendment, since it unreasonably restrained his freedom of speech, freedom of the press, and freedom of worship.

Chaplinsky's claims were overruled. A state court found him guilty. Chaplinsky's appeals to state appellate courts failed. Eventually his case reached the U.S. Supreme Court, which handed down its ruling on March 9, 1942.

The ruling went against Chaplinsky. The majority opinion was written by Justice Frank Murphy. To help explain the Court's reasoning, he wrote:

> There are certain well-defined and narrowly limited classes of speech, the prevention and punishment of which has never been thought to raise any Constitutional problem. These include the lewd and obscene, the profane, the libelous, and the insulting or "fighting" words—those which by their very utterance inflict injury or tend to incite an immediate breach of the peace. It has been well observed that such utterances are no essential part of any exposition of ideas, and are of such slight social value as a step to truth that any benefit that may be derived from them is clearly outweighed by the social interest in order and morality.

That is, if the speaker is genuinely focused on making his views known through his words, his speech has social value and is protected. But if, instead, he is determined to use his words to provoke a physical fight, then his words are no longer seen as having social value or as being acceptable to most people. And so the government is entitled to limit his right to freedom of speech to prevent a breach of the peace.

The *Eichman* justices would look closely at this ruling and compare Chaplinsky's actions with those of the *Eichman* flag burners. The *Chaplinsky* ruling would help the justices decide whether the flag burners' actions constituted a threat to law and order.

Free Speech Precedent:
Terminiello V. *CITY OF CHICAGO*

Another precedent case focuses on the clear and present danger and fighting words tests as limits to freedom of speech. In this case from 1949 a Catholic priest named Father Arthur Terminiello delivered a vicious speech in a Chicago auditorium. His targets were various political groups. His words included slurs aimed at ethnic and religious groups. As he spoke, a crowd of protesters gathered outside. They couldn't get in because the auditorium was filled to capacity, with more than eight hundred people present.

The protesters became angry and unruly to the point of throwing things. A crowd of policemen attempted to keep order, but there were several outbreaks of violence, and Terminiello was arrested for breach of the peace. The city ordinance defined *breach of the peace* as misbehavior that "stirs the public to anger, invites dispute, brings about a condition of unrest, or creates a disturbance, or . . . molests the inhabitants in the enjoyment of peace and quiet by arousing alarm."

At his trial Terminiello insisted that the city ordinance was unconstitutional, since it violated his First Amendment right of free speech. Terminiello was prosecuted for using fighting words that presented a clear and present danger and, thus, put his conduct outside the protections of the First Amendment. He was found guilty for his central role in inciting a riot.

Peace versus Speech

The case worked its way through the appeals system until it got to the U.S. Supreme Court. The question before the Court was whether the Chicago ordinance violated Terminiello's right of free expression, guaranteed by the First Amendment.

SUPREME COURT JUSTICE WILLIAM O. DOUGLAS VOTED CONSISTENTLY IN FAVOR OF FREE SPEECH. IN 1949, HE WROTE THE MAJORITY OPINION IN *TERMINIELLO*, WRITING THAT DISPUTE IS AN ESSENTIAL ASPECT OF FREEDOM.

The Court's 5 to 4 ruling, handed down on May 16, 1949, was in favor of Terminiello. In the majority opinion Justice William O. Douglas wrote that "a function of free speech under our system is to invite dispute. It may indeed best serve its high purpose when it induces a condition of unrest, creates dissatisfaction with conditions as they are, or even stirs people to anger."

So although Terminiello's words stirred people to anger and even to rioting, those words were protected by the First Amendment. Why? The Court found that, unlike Chaplinsky's fighting words, which were purely personal, directed squarely at provoking one particular person, Terminiello's vicious anger was impersonal, aimed at criticizing political institutions rather than starting a fistfight.

The importance of these cases

As *Schenck* and *Chaplinsky* show, free speech has its limits in regard to clear and present danger and fighting words. Schenck's free speech rights were limited because his words posed a threat to U.S. security in a time of war. Chaplinsky's rights were limited because rather than protesting government policies, he was trying to pick a fight.

But as *Terminiello* shows, those limits to free speech have limits of their own. The *Eichman* justices would compare Terminiello's anti-ethnic and antireligious slurs with the *Eichman* flag burners' actions. They would note that in both cases, the defendants had expressed ideas that were deeply offensive to society. But they would also note that, in the case of *Terminiello*, the fact that those ideas were offensive did not necessarily mean that the government could prohibit their expression.

Where, in all of this, did the Eichman flag burners' actions fall? Did they constitute a clear and present danger or fighting words? Were they so offensive to common decency that they should be seen as criminal? Sometimes it's a fine line that divides protected speech from unprotected speech, a line that the justices would have to draw thoughtfully in deciding *Eichman*.

Not everyone uses the flag to protest *against* the United States, or its wars. This elderly veteran holds a flag and wears a sign with a flag on it reading "God Bless America."

FIVE
HONORING THE FLAG

SQUARELY AT THE center OF *EICHMAN* was the U.S. flag itself—Old Glory, a most powerful and controversial symbol. When people disrespect the flag, their actions are liable to stir up the "condition of unrest" that Justice Douglas mentioned in the *Terminiello* opinion. Many people see the flag as a cherished symbol of all that the United States stands for, and seeing that cherished symbol set afire may upset them deeply.

Shows of disrespect for the flag may also stir people to anger and inspire a passionately protective feeling toward the flag. In addition to precedents dealing with free speech, the *Eichman* justices would draw upon the history of flag protection to help decide the case. In particular they would look at the Flag Protection Act of 1989 in relation to past laws meant to protect the flag.

FLAG PROTECTION PRECEDENT: *HALTER V. NEBRASKA*

Starting in 1897 states began passing laws to protect the flag. Illinois, Pennsylvania, and South Dakota were the first states to pass laws outlawing flag desecration. To desecrate an object is to violate its sacred character in some way. Often this involves physical destruction, such as tearing or burning. Eventually forty-eight states would pass similar laws. Only Alaska and Wyoming did not.

People also wanted to protect the flag from what they saw as commercial desecration, exploiting this sacred symbol by using it to sell a product. The first case to deal with commercial flag desecration came before the Court in 1907. Halter, a beer manufacturer in Nebraska, had been selling "Stars and Stripes" beer, with a U.S. flag printed on the label.

Nebraska had a statute on the books that made it a crime "for anyone to sell, expose for sale, or have in possession for sale, any article of merchandise upon which shall have been printed or placed, for purposes of advertisement, a representation of the flag of the United States."

A SACRED SYMBOL

Halter and the other plaintiffs from the beer company were found guilty of violating this act. They appealed, asking that the Nebraska statute be declared unconstitutional for depriving them of their liberty guaranteed by the Fourteenth Amendment. The law, they claimed, was denying them their property rights in regard to the beer.

The case eventually reached the U.S. Supreme Court. On March 14, 1907, the Court ruled in favor of the state of Nebraska. Justice John M. Harlan wrote the unanimous opinion.

The significance of this case as a precedent for *Eichman* lies in what Justice Harlan's opinion said about the flag itself, which he called "the emblem of the American Republic":

> For that flag every true American has not simply an appreciation, but a deep affection. No American, nor any foreign-born person who enjoys the privileges of American citizenship, ever looks upon it without taking pride in the fact that he lives under this free government. Hence, it has often occurred

that insults to a flag have been the cause of war, and indignities put upon it, in the presence of those who revere it, have often been resented and sometimes punished on the spot.

The opinion went on to state plainly what the Court thought about passing laws to protect the flag from those who would desecrate it:

When, by its legislation, the state encourages a feeling of patriotism towards the nation, it necessarily encourages a like feeling towards the state. One who loves the Union will love the state in which he resides, and love both of the common country and of the state will diminish in proportion as respect for the flag is weakened. Therefore a state will be wanting in care for the well-being of its people if it ignores the fact that they regard the flag as a symbol of their country's power and prestige, and will be impatient if any open disrespect is shown towards it.

In other words this Court unanimously regarded the flag as a symbol vital for the preservation of the nation's well-being and saw those who disrespected it as deserving of punishment. When the *Eichman* justices looked back at *Halter*, it would show them a vivid example of how passionately past justices felt at the beginning of the twentieth century about protecting the flag from the kind of desecration inflicted upon it by the *Eichman* flag burners.

FREE SPEECH PRECEDENT: *MINERSVILLE SCHOOL DISTRICT V. GOBITIS*

Halter dealt with the crime of desecrating the flag, which the *Eichman* flag burners also had done. The next two cases dealt with refusing to honor the flag. What did past Court decisions have to say about this offense?

In the case of *Minersville School District* v. *Gobitis* (1940), school officials expelled two students attending school in Minersville, Pennsylvania, for refusing to salute the flag by extending the right arm, palm upward, and recite the Pledge of Allegiance: "I pledge allegiance to the flag of the United States of America and to the Republic for which it stands; one Nation, indivisible, with liberty and justice for all."

World War II was raging in Europe. The United States would not actually join the fighting until December 7, 1941, after the Japanese air force attacked the U.S. naval fleet at Pearl Harbor, Hawaii. But a strong scent of war was in the air, and any action that appeared to dishonor the flag would likely be condemned as unpatriotic.

But the students—Lillian Gobitas (the name was misspelled in the court case), age twelve, and her brother William, ten—refused to recite the pledge due to religious convictions. The pledge asks that the speaker swear allegiance to the flag and to the republic for which it stands. But the students were Jehovah's Witnesses. Their religion forbade swearing loyalty to any power except God.

Lillian and William Gobitas believed they were free to sit quietly while the other students recited the pledge. After all, the First Amendment guaranteed their right to freedom of religion. School officials disagreed and expelled them for refusing to participate in a daily school exercise.

FREEDOM VERSUS RESPONSIBILITY

The Gobitas family challenged the expulsions. Here was a freedom of speech case that was different from the others decided so far. Instead of claiming their right to express themselves freely, the defendants in this case were claiming their right to withhold their expression.

The case ended up in the U.S. Supreme Court. On June 3, 1940, Justice Felix Frankfurter delivered the majority opinion. He stated the question before the Court this way: "We must decide whether the requirement of participation in such a ceremony, exacted from a child who refuses upon sincere religious grounds, infringes without due process of law the liberty guaranteed by the Fourteenth Amendment."

Here was a classic clash between an individual citizen's need to act in accordance with religious beliefs and the nation's need for citizens to express their secular patriotism. Which need should come first? In the Court's opinion, the answer was duty to the nation. Justice Frankfurter wrote, "The mere possession of religious convictions which contradict the relevant concerns of a political society does not relieve the citizen from the discharge of political responsibilities."

And so the Minersville school district won the case by a vote of 8 to 1. But a decision in another case would soon overturn this ruling.

Free Speech Precedent: *West Virginia Board of Education* v. *Barnette*

In 1945, only three years after *Minersville*, a nearly identical case made its way to the Court, this time with distinctly different results. The West Virginia State Board of Education required all students to recite the Pledge of Allegiance. The regulation stated that "refusal to salute the Flag [will] be regarded as an Act of insubordination, and shall be dealt with accordingly."

Not surprisingly, the same things happened there as happened in *Minersville*. Students who were Jehovah's Witnesses were expelled when they refused to recite the pledge. In addition, they could be sent to reformatories for juvenile lawbreakers, and their parents could be prosecuted for contributing to the delinquency of their children. The expelled children's parents filed suit, claiming that the regulation amounted to a denial of the First Amendment freedoms of speech and religion. The lawsuit also charged that the West Virginia regulation was invalid under the due process and equal protection clauses of the Fourteenth Amendment.

THE *WEST VIRGINIA* RULING
On June 14, 1943, Justice Robert H. Jackson delivered the opinion of the Court. Here he focused on the "clear and present danger" test:

> [C]ensorship or suppression of expression of opinion is tolerated by our Constitution only when the expression presents a clear and present danger of action of a kind the State is empowered to prevent and punish. . . . But here the power of compulsion is invoked without any allegation that remaining passive during a flag salute ritual creates a clear and present danger that would justify an effort even to muffle expression. To sustain the compulsory flag salute we are required to say that a Bill of Rights which guards the individual's right to speak his own mind, left it open to public authorities to compel him to utter what is not in his mind.

In other words, the children who were sitting quietly as the pledge was recited clearly did not constitute a "clear and present danger." Also, free speech meant not only the freedom to speak one's mind but the freedom to remain silent as well. And so the Court ruled in favor of the students, reversing its earlier ruling in *Minersville*:

THE FLAG CONTINUES TO BE A POTENT SOURCE OF PROTEST, WHATEVER THE COURTS DECIDE. ON THE EVE OF THE 2000 REPUBLICAN PRESIDENTIAL CONVENTION IN PHILADELPHIA, "SALLY FUTURES" GAGGED HERSELF WITH AN UPSIDE-DOWN AMERICAN FLAG TO PROTEST REPUBLICAN PARTY POLICIES.

We think the action of the local authorities in compelling the flag salute and pledge transcends constitutional limitations on their power and invades the sphere of intellect and spirit which it is the purpose of the First Amendment to our Constitution to reserve from all official control.

FLAG HISTORY HIGHLIGHTS

On June 14, 1777, the Continental Congress passed the first Flag Act: "Resolved, That the flag of the United States be made of thirteen stripes, alternate red and white; that the union be thirteen stars, white in a blue field, representing a new Constellation."

On April 4, 1818, President James Monroe signed another flag act stating that there now would be a total of thirteen stripes and a single star for each state. For each new state admitted to the Union, a star would added on the following July 4.

On January 3, 1959, when the forty-ninth state, Alaska, was admitted to the Union, President Dwight Eisenhower issued an executive order stating that the stars would be arranged in seven rows of seven stars each.

On August 21, 1959, when the fiftieth state, Hawaii, was admitted, President Eisenhower issued another executive order stating that the stars would now be arranged in five rows of six stars alternating with four rows of five stars.

The fifty-star flag was the brainchild of Robert G. Heft, a high school student from Lancaster, Ohio. Heft created it for a school project. His teacher gave him a B minus, saying that the design was not very creative. But the teacher offered to raise the grade if Heft could get his design adopted by Congress.

"When I was in school I was really shy," Heft said, thinking back. "I was always the type of kid to sit in the back of the class." But he wasn't shy about his flag design. He sent it to his congressional representative, and eventually it became the nation's fifty-star flag.

Factors to Consider

Looking back at *Minersville* and *West Virginia*, the *Eichman* justices would see one factor that favored the petitioner's case: the reversal of precedent. It was rare for the Court to reverse one of its own rulings, but it was not unheard of. In *Eichman* the government was asking the justices to reverse their *Johnson* ruling, and *West Virginia* reminded them that there was a precedent to honor that request.

But another factor favored the respondents' case. In *West Virginia* the Court had extended the limits of free speech in regard to honoring, or choosing not to honor, the flag. In *Minersville* (1940) the Court ruled that when you found that your responsibilities as a good citizen were at odds with your First Amendment freedoms, you ought to accept the limits the state puts on those freedoms, no matter what. But in *West Virginia* (1943) the Court ruled that First Amendment freedoms may be restricted "only to prevent grave and immediate danger to interests which the state may lawfully protect."

The *Eichman* justices also would see how, through the years, the Court has taken differing views of the U.S. flag. In *Halter* (1907) the Court saw the flag as "a symbol of [the] country's power and prestige" and mentioned the public's impatience with "any open disrespect . . . shown towards it." But in *West Virginia* (1943) the Court saw the flag from another perspective: "A person gets from a symbol the meaning he puts into it, and what is one man's comfort and inspiration is another's jest and scorn." These factors would all come into play when the justices pondered their vote in *Eichman*.

CIVIL RIGHTS ACTIVIST JAMES MEREDITH WAS SHOT ON THE SECOND DAY OF THE 1966 CIVIL RIGHTS MARCH AGAINST FEAR. HE REJOINED THE MARCH AFTER HE RECOVERED FROM THE SNIPER'S WOUND.

SIX
DESECRATING THE FLAG

Halter was the first U.S. Supreme Court case dealing with flag desecration, and it involved commercial use—using the flag to sell something. What about flag desecration cases such as *Eichman*, in which defendants were tried for desecrating the flag by showing contempt for it? The *Eichman* justices would be looking closely at those precedent cases to help them make their decision. The first one occurred during the Vietnam War.

vietnam protests

As the Vietnam War dragged on through the 1960s, it became increasingly unpopular. More and more people protested and demonstrated against it, including David Paul O'Brien in *United States* v. *O'Brien* (1968) and the students in *Tinker* v. *Des Moines* (1969). From 1963 to 1975, 9,118 men were prosecuted for refusing to be drafted into the armed forces, including heavyweight boxing champion Muhammad Ali.

One of the protesters' more controversial tactics for getting their message across was flag burning. An April 1967 demonstration in New York's Central Park, for instance, received national attention. Antiwar protesters chanted "Hell no, we won't go!" and burned an American flag.

In 1968 Congress reacted to the flag burnings by passing a federal flag protection act: "Whoever knowingly casts contempt upon any flag of the United States by publicly mutilating, defacing, defiling, burning, or trampling upon it shall be fined not more than $1,000 or imprisoned for not more than one year, or both."

For the next two decades only three cases involving the 1968 statute reached the U.S. Supreme Court: *Street* v. *New York* (1969), *Smith* v. *Goguen* (1974), and *Spence* v. *Washington* (1974). All three cases took place during the Vietnam War, and all three would serve as precedents for the *Eichman* justices.

Free Speech Precedent: *Street* v. *New York*

On June 6, 1966, law student and civil rights leader James Meredith was leading a march from Tennessee to Mississippi as part of a black voter-registration drive when he was wounded by a sniper. That same day Bronze Star recipient and civil rights activist Sidney Street heard the news on the radio in his Brooklyn, New York, apartment.

Street, like Meredith, was African American, and he was outraged at the news. "They didn't protect him," Street said to himself. Then he opened a drawer and took out a neatly folded American flag that he had displayed on national holidays. He carried the flag, still folded, to a nearby intersection, lit it with a match, and dropped it to the pavement, where it began to burn. Street was arrested and charged with malicious mischief for violating a New York state statute that made it a crime publicly to mutilate or "publicly [to] defy . . . or cast contempt upon [any American flag] either by words or act."

The arresting officer said that Street stood on a corner speaking to a small group of people while, on the opposite corner, the flag burned. "We don't need no damn flag," Street said to the officer. "If they let that happen to Meredith, we don't need an American flag."

After being tried and convicted, Street received a

suspended sentence. He appealed the conviction, citing the phrase "either by words or act" in the statute. He said that convicting him for his "words" was a violation of his First Amendment rights. New York appeals courts upheld the conviction. Then the case was accepted by the U.S. Supreme Court for review.

Freedom to Differ

The Court handed down its ruling on April 21, 1969. The majority opinion was delivered by Justice John Marshall Harlan. The Court found in favor of Street.

In the majority opinion Justice Harlan cited *Halter* v. *Nebraska* (1907) and wrote, "[D]isrespect for our flag is to be deplored no less in these vexed times than in calmer periods of our history. Nevertheless, we are unable to sustain a conviction that may have rested on a form of expression, however distasteful, which the Constitution tolerates and protects."

Justice Harlan also cited as precedent *West Virginia* v. *Barnette* (1943) and quoted from that opinion as well:

> The case is made difficult not because the principles of its decision are obscure but because the flag involved is our own. Nevertheless, we apply the limitations of the Constitution with no fear that freedom to be intellectually and spiritually diverse or even contrary will disintegrate the social organization. . . . [F]reedom to differ is not limited to things that do not matter much. That would be a mere shadow of freedom. The test of its substance is the right to differ as to things that touch the heart of the existing order.

By quoting these passages from *Halter* and *West Virginia*, Justice Harlan made it clear that in *Street*, as in those earlier cases, the justices were not condoning the desecration of the U.S. flag. In fact they were opposed to flag desecration. But their personal opposition had to take a backseat to the freedom of speech granted to citizens by the U.S. Constitution, the freedom to express highly unpopular ideas through highly unpopular, even abhorrent, words and actions. The argument for the *Eichman* respondents was strengthened by the quotations from *Halter* and *West Virginia*.

But the case for the *Eichman* petitioners would be aided by a dissenting opinion. Justice Hugo Black, who dissented in the *West Virginia* and *Tinker* cases, dissented here as well. His decision came as a surprise, since Justice Black, who served on the Court from 1937 to 1971, was a leading upholder of First Amendment rights. In his *Street* dissent Justice Black wrote:

> It passes my belief that anything in the Federal Constitution bars a State from making the deliberate burning of the American flag an offense. It is immaterial to me that words are spoken in connection with the burning. It is the burning of the flag that the State has set its face against.

In other words, Justice Black said, it does not matter what words of political protest the flag burner writes or speaks. It is the physical burning of the flag, apart from any symbolic expression, that ought to be subject to punishment—the precise point that the petitioners, the government, were making in the *Eichman* case.

FREE SPEECH PRECEDENT: *SMITH* V. *GOGUEN*

On January 30, 1970, two police officers in Leominster, Massachusetts, saw Goguen wearing a small cloth version of the U.S. flag sewn on the seat of his blue jeans, on the left.

The flag was about four inches by six inches. He was arrested for violating a Massachusetts statute that read in part:

> Whoever publicly mutilates, tramples upon, defaces or treats contemptuously the flag of the United States . . . whether such flag is public or private property . . . , shall be punished by a fine of not less than ten nor more than one hundred dollars or by imprisonment for not more than one year, or both. . . .

Goguen was not charged with physical desecration of the flag. He was charged only with violating the part of the statute dealing with treating the flag "contemptuously." He was found guilty and sentenced to six months in the Massachusetts house of corrections.

Goguen appealed the conviction on the grounds that the statute was vague, with no definitions or examples of what was meant by "treats contemptuously the flag of the United States." Appeals courts agreed and reversed the conviction. The state of Massachusetts appealed those decisions to the U.S. Supreme Court, which agreed to hear the case.

Fashion Statement

The Court's ruling was handed down on March 25, 1974, in an opinion written by Justice Lewis Powell. By a 6 to 3 vote the Court found in favor of Goguen.

What one man may consider contemptuous, the opinion said, may be a work of art to another. Although some would not consider the patch art, it could not be seen as contemptuous, since wearing the flag had become a fashion statement:

> Flag wearing in a day of relaxed clothing styles may be simply for adornment or a ploy to attract

attention. It and many other current, careless uses of the flag nevertheless constitute unceremonial treatment that many people may view as contemptuous. Yet in a time of widely varying attitudes and tastes for displaying something as ubiquitous as the United States flag or representations of it, it could hardly be the purpose of the Massachusetts Legislature to make criminal every informal use of the flag.

Here was an opinion with a new point of view about the flag, based on a new public attitude. Now that so many people were wearing representations of the flag as clothing, community standards had changed. Although the flag was still a sacred symbol to many, it clearly was not so to others.

And yet those others did not hold the flag in contempt. They simply did not feel it was wrong to use the flag as something other than a sacred symbol of the nation. And so punishing people such as Goguen for exhibiting this new public attitude was not appropriate.

concurrence anD DiSSenT

Justices who agree with the majority opinion for somewhat different reasons may offer their point of view in a concurring opinion. In his concurrence, Justice Byron White wrote that a conviction for treating the flag with contempt would punish the communication of ideas and therefore would be a First Amendment violation.

And what about the dissenting justices? All three believed that the state had a clear interest in preserving the flag's physical integrity. Justice William Rehnquist went so far as to declare that even someone who buys a flag for personal use should be prohibited from desecrating it. "For what they have purchased is not merely cloth dyed

same FLAG, DIFFERENT SYMBOL

The flag can carry distinctly different meanings for different people. Bob Kerrey, a Nebraska senator, attended a military funeral at Arlington National Cemetery in Arlington, Virginia. Veterans from all the nation's wars are buried there, from the American Revolution through the war in Iraq.

During the ceremony, an honor guard holds the American flag. The guards then fold it into a triangle and hand it to the buried soldier's next of kin. Kerrey wrote, "At that moment the American flag is a sacred object that holds the sweet memory of a life given to a higher cause. Or so it seems to me each time I am witness to these hallowed events."

Not everyone whose loved one has been killed feels that way, though. For some it means the loss of a loved one in a meaningless war. Kerrey wrote, "A mother of a friend who was killed in Vietnam recoiled when the flag was offered to her. She would not take it. In her heart the American flag had become a symbol of dishonor, treachery and betrayal."

red, white and blue, but also the visible manifestation of two hundred years of nationhood," he wrote.

Free speech precedent: *Spence* v. *Washington*

On May 10, 1970, Harold Spence, a student at the University of Washington, hung his U.S. flag from the window of his apartment. This would not have gotten him into trouble with the law except for two things: he hung the flag upside down, and he attached a peace symbol to it, made of removable black tape. The peace symbol, a trident inside a circle, was originally a symbol for nuclear disarmament. During the Vietnam War it also became a symbol for ending that war. Spence's peace symbol took up about half of the flag's total surface.

Three Seattle police officers spotted the flag and entered the building. They seized the flag and arrested Spence, who put up no resistance. Spence was convicted under a state statute that forbade exhibiting a U.S. flag that had other figures or symbols attached to it. At his trial Spence testified that he had displayed the flag as a protest against recent U.S. bombings in Cambodia, a nation bordering Vietnam, and an incident at Kent State University, in Kent, Ohio, in which National Guardsmen shot at student war protesters, killing four and wounding nine.

Spence testified that he hung up the U.S. flag with the peace symbol attached to associate it with peace instead of war and violence. "I felt there had been so much killing and that this was not what America stood for. I felt that the flag stood for America and I wanted people to know that I thought America stood for peace," he said.

APPLYING precedent

Spence was convicted. On appeal he contended that the statute denied him his rights under the First and Fourteenth amendments. The Washington State Supreme Court disagreed and upheld the conviction. The case reached the U.S. Supreme Court, which handed down its ruling on June 25, 1974. The majority opinion was written *per curiam*, an unsigned opinion, usually short opinions given when cases are not seen as particularly controversial. The Court ruled in favor of Spence and reversed his conviction. Looking back at action-as-speech precedent, the justices ruled that attaching a peace sign to a flag was a form of constitutionally protected speech:

> [T]his was not an act of mindless nihilism. Rather, it was a pointed expression of anguish by appellant [Spence] about the then-current domestic and foreign affairs of his government. An intent to convey a particularized message was present, and in the surrounding circumstances the likelihood was great that the message would be understood by those who viewed it.

Stromberg v. *California* and *West Virginia* v. *Barnette* were also brought into play. The Court referred to *Stromberg* in stating that, for decades, the flag had carried symbolic meaning. It referred to *West Virginia* in saying that the flag symbolized patriotism for some people while for others it carried a different message. "[T]here can be little doubt that [Spence] communicated through the use of symbols. The symbolism included not only the flag but also the superimposed peace symbol."

Then there was the issue of dangerous words. Quoting from *Street* v. *New York*, the Court wrote, "It is firmly settled under our Constitution that the public expression of ideas may not be prohibited merely because the ideas are themselves offensive to some of their hearers." The Court added, "Moreover, [Spence] did not impose his ideas upon a captive audience. Anyone who might have been offended could easily have avoided the display."

Applying the O'Brien test, the Court rejected the state's argument that promoting respect for the flag and preserving it as a symbol of the nation were important interests unrelated to the suppression of free speech. Although the state did have a real interest in punishing the improper use of government-owned flags, it could not show that same interest for the improper use of a privately owned flag.

DISSENTING VOICES

Justice William Rehnquist disagreed. Chief Justice Warren Burger and Justice Byron White joined in Rehnquist's dissenting opinion. Rehnquist saw Spence's lower-court conviction as a reasonable limitation to freedom of speech:

> The Court has further recognized that even protected speech may be subject to reasonable limitation when important countervailing interests are involved. Citizens are not completely free to commit perjury, to libel other citizens, to infringe copyrights, to incite riots, or to interfere unduly with passage through a public thoroughfare. The right of free speech, though precious, remains subject to reasonable accommodation to other valued interests.

Although the outcome of *Spence* would be seen as supporting the respondents in *Eichman*, Rehnquist's dissent would be seen as supporting the petitioners.

WHY *STREET*, *GOGUEN*, AND *SPENCE* ARE IMPORTANT

All three of these precedent cases involved flag desecration. For that reason they would play prominent roles in the *Eichman* ruling.

All three rulings found in favor of the individual and against the state and federal government. But there was plenty of disagreement. Determined dissenting opinions were delivered in all three cases. And based on the opinions,

WILLIAM H. REHNQUIST'S APPOINTMENT AS CHIEF JUSTICE OF THE SUPREME COURT MARKED A CONSERVATIVE SHIFT TO THE DEBATE OVER USING FLAG DESECRATION AS A FORM OF SYMBOLIC SPEECH.

both majority and dissenting, it was clear that a justice's personal feelings about the U.S. flag could influence which way the justice would vote.

The most important precedent-setting case was yet to come, however. It would set the stage for a controversial new federal statute to protect the flag and a fresh wave of flag desecrations that would lead to *Eichman*.

Inside the 1984 Republican National Convention hall in Dallas, Texas, supporters celebrated the renomination of President Ronald Reagan; outside, demonstrators protested.

seven
TEXAS V. JOHNSON

IN 1984 THE REPUBLICAN PARTY held its National Convention in Dallas, Texas, during which it renominated President Ronald Reagan for a second term. Outside the convention center demonstrators marched to protest the policies of President Reagan and some Dallas-based corporations.

One of the demonstrators was Gregory Lee Johnson. Johnson belonged to the Revolutionary Communist Youth Brigade, whose members often wore T-shirts that showed a large red star and the silhouette of a young person raising a rifle. Also on the shirt was the anti-American message "I was born in the sewer called capitalism but now I'm living for revolution!"

The demonstrators marched through the city streets, chanting slogans and staging die-ins to dramatize the deadly consequences of nuclear war. In a die-in, protesters lie on the ground and pretend to be dead. Sometimes bandages are added for the sake of realism, painted to look as if they cover bleeding wounds.

BURNING THE FLAG
At one point during the march a fellow protester handed Johnson an American flag that had been taken from a flagpole outside a building. When the demonstration reached Dallas's city hall, Johnson unfurled the flag, threw

kerosene on it, and set it afire, while demonstrators chanted, "America, the red, white, and blue, we spit on you." Some bystanders were angered and offended by the sight of the burning flag. One took its remains home and buried them in his backyard. There were shouts of anger but no outbreaks of violence during the demonstration. Out of the one hundred or so demonstrators, only Johnson was arrested and charged with a crime. He was charged with violating the Texas flag-desecration statute.

JOHNSON'S TRIALS

Johnson was convicted in a Texas state court of "intentionally or knowingly [desecrating] a state or national flag." His sentence was a year in prison and a two-thousand-dollar fine.

Johnson appealed the conviction on the grounds that it was unconstitutional. A state court of appeals upheld the trial court's conviction. It agreed that Johnson's flag burning was expressive conduct protected by the First Amendment. But it claimed two overriding state interests: preserving the flag as a symbol of national unity and preventing breaches of the peace.

Johnson appealed the state court ruling to the Texas Court of Criminal Appeals, claiming that the conviction for flag burning violated his First Amendment rights. The Texas Court of Criminal Appeals agreed and reversed the lower court decision, ruling that it was inconsistent with the First Amendment and therefore unconstitutional. The appeals court also ruled that neither of the state's claims of overriding interest supported the conviction.

INTERPRETING THE CONSTITUTION

The state of Texas appealed the Court of Criminal Appeals's ruling to the U.S. Supreme Court. The case was argued on March 21, 1989.

To decide *Johnson*, the justices would have to interpret the U.S. Constitution. Although many government documents attempt to be precise, the Constitution is deliberately general and vague. It was meant to serve as an enduring foundation, but a foundation only. It was meant to be interpreted. Since interpretation is to some degree a personal matter, the Court's decisions are influenced by its makeup. Each justice looks at the issues from his or her personal point of view, influenced by his or her political beliefs. The justices apply their own sets of beliefs and feelings to the constitutional questions at hand.

Some justices are seen as progressives or activists. They tend to be more liberal in interpreting the Constitution, as long as these interpretations reflect what they see as the Founding Fathers' vision for the nation. Supreme Court expert and author Jan Crawford Greenburg summed up the liberal justices' position this way:

> The Court was supposed to protect the rights of the minority against the will of the majority. . . . That approach encouraged the justices to identify new constitutional rights, especially in situations the document's framers could never have imagined two hundred years earlier. As society changed, the understanding of the Constitution should change with it, liberals believed, and the justices should help foster the progression.

Other justices are seen as strict constructionists. When it comes to interpreting the Constitution, they tend to be more conservative. If the answer to a question before the Court is not contained in the Constitution itself, then, in their opinion, that question must be left to the individual states to decide. They tend to support states' rights over federal rights.

Greenburg summed up the conservative justices' position this way:

> Conservatives saw a Supreme Court that had arrogantly grabbed power for itself. By deciding those issues and creating new constitutional rights, conservatives believed, the [liberal] justices usurped the role of elected officials, who were closer to the people and more accountable for their decisions at the ballot box. That struck at the heart of democratic participation, they believed.

THE REHNQUIST COURT

U.S. Supreme Court justices are appointed for life. When a justice retires or dies, a new justice is appointed to fill the vacancy. The president does the appointing. Conservative-minded presidents tend to appoint conservative justices; liberal-minded presidents tend to appoint liberal justices.

Together, the nine justices who ruled on *Texas* v. *Johnson* were known as the Rehnquist Court. Chief Justice Rehnquist and Justices Antonin Scalia, Anthony Kennedy, Byron White, and Sandra Day O'Connor were considered the Court's conservatives. The remaining justices—Thurgood Marshall, Harry Blackmun, William Brennan Jr., and John Paul Stevens—were considered the Court's liberals.

Looking at the *Johnson* case strictly from the liberal-versus-conservative viewpoint, the Court most likely would have ruled in favor of the state of Texas by a 5 to 4 vote. However, another factor came into play: U.S. Supreme Court justices are not always predictable. Justice Sandra Day O'Connor, the Court's first woman member, for instance, while generally conservative, sometimes sided with liberals on social issues. And Justice Antonin Scalia, a strict constructionist as a rule, has been called "the ever-unpredictable justice."

THE NINE JUSTICES WHO RULED ON *TEXAS* V. *JOHNSON* WERE KNOWN AS THE REHNQUIST COURT. SITTING (L TO R): THURGOOD MARSHALL, WILLIAM BRENNAN JR., CHIEF JUSTICE WILLIAM REHNQUIST, BYRON WHITE, AND HARRY BLACKMUN. STANDING (L TO R): ANTONIN SCALIA, JOHN PAUL STEVENS, SANDRA DAY O'CONNOR, AND ANTHONY KENNEDY.

THE JOHNSON RULING

On June 21, 1989, the ruling was handed down. Although the vote was 5 to 4, it was not in favor of the state of Texas trial court ruling that had found Johnson guilty. Instead, the Court ruled in favor of Johnson:

> After publicly burning an American flag as a
> means of political protest, Gregory Lee Johnson

was convicted of desecrating a flag in violation of Texas law. This case presents the question whether his conviction is consistent with the First Amendment. We hold that it is not.

Conservatives Scalia and Kennedy joined liberals Marshall, Blackmun, and Brennan, while the liberal Stevens sided with dissenters O'Connor, Rehnquist, and White. Justice Brennan wrote the majority opinion. To show how high passions ran on this issue, four opinions were written in all: two siding with the majority and two in dissent. The opinions show that the justices held very different and distinct views on how the Court ought to interpret the Constitution.

Here, from the majority opinion, is a summary of the Court's reasoning:

> Johnson was convicted for engaging in expressive conduct. The State's interest in preventing breaches of the peace does not support his conviction, because Johnson's conduct did not threaten to disturb the peace. Nor does the State's interest in preserving the flag as a symbol of nationhood and national unity justify his criminal conviction for engaging in political expression. The judgment of the Texas Court of Criminal Appeals is therefore Affirmed.

There is a sports-based saying that goes "No harm, no foul." In other words, although Johnson's actions might have caused a breach of the peace, they did not. Nor had he intended them to. His actions did not present a clear and present danger, nor did they constitute fighting words. And while the state of Texas had the right to protect the flag's symbolic value, it did not have the right to do so at the price of depriving Johnson of his First Amendment right to freedom of expression.

expressive conduct

Now let's examine the Court's reasoning in more detail. The majority opinion listed the questions that needed to be addressed in a First Amendment case like this one, where conduct and actions rather than "pure speech" were at issue. The first question was: "We must first determine whether Johnson's burning of the flag constituted expressive conduct, permitting him to invoke the First Amendment in challenging his conviction."

The test of whether conduct is expressive enough to call for First Amendment protections relies on two factors: whether "[a]n intent to convey a particularized message was present, and [whether] the likelihood was great that the message would be understood by those who viewed it."

The justices looked back at precedents. They cited *Tinker* v. *Des Moines:* "[W]e have recognized the expressive nature of students' wearing of black armbands to protest American military involvement in Vietnam." They also cited *Schacht* v. *United States:* "the wearing of American military uniforms in a dramatic presentation criticizing American involvement in Vietnam...."

They looked at decisions that recognized the communicative nature of conduct relating to flags. These included *Spence* v. *Washington* ("[a]ttaching a peace sign to the flag"), *West Virginia* v. *Barnette* ("refusing to salute the flag"), *Stromberg* v. *California* ("displaying a red flag"), and *Smith* v. *Goguen* ("treating the flag 'contemptuously' by wearing pants with small flag sewn into their seat").

FLaGs as symBoLs

From these cases the Court concluded, "[W]e have had little difficulty identifying an expressive element in conduct relating to flags. . . . Pregnant with expressive content, the flag as readily signifies this Nation as does the combination of letters found in 'America.'"

Then, the Court gave a caution and another test:

> We have not automatically concluded, however, that any action taken with respect to our flag is expressive. Instead . . . we have considered the context in which it occurred. In *Spence*, for example, we emphasized that Spence's taping of a peace sign to his flag was "roughly simultaneous with and concededly triggered by the Cambodian incursion and the Kent State tragedy."

That is, Spence's expressive actions with the flag were part of a genuine political protest against U.S. government policies. Therefore they deserved First Amendment protections. And did the context of Johnson's conduct pass this same test? The Court said yes, it did:

> Johnson burned an American flag as part—indeed, as the culmination—of a political demonstration that coincided with the convening of the Republican Party and its renomination of Ronald Reagan for President. The expressive, overtly political nature of this conduct was both intentional and overwhelmingly apparent. . . . In these circumstances, Johnson's burning of the flag was conduct "sufficiently imbued with elements of communication," [quoting from *Spence*] to implicate the First Amendment.

APPLYING THE O'BRIEN TEST

Now for the second question the Court addressed: "If his conduct was expressive, we next decide whether the

DISTASTEFUL DECISIONS

Sometimes justices must set aside their personal feelings and make decisions they would rather not have to make. In his concurring opinion in *Texas* v. *Johnson*, Justice Anthony Kennedy wrote:

> The hard fact is that sometimes we must make decisions we do not like. We make them because they are right, right in the sense that the law and the Constitution, as we see them, compel the result. And so great is our commitment to the process that, except in the rare case, we do not pause to express distaste for the result, perhaps for fear of undermining a valued principle that dictates the decision. This is one of those rare cases.

In his concurring opinion, Justice Kennedy took pains to make it plain what he thought of flag burning: that it was morally reprehensible in the extreme. But he also knew that, as a member of the Court, it was his overriding duty to protect and uphold the U.S. Constitution, even if it meant, as it did here, protecting a man who had committed what Kennedy saw as a morally reprehensible act.

State's regulation is related to the suppression of free expression."

The authorities could not suppress Johnson's right to free speech simply because they objected to his message. But they might be able to suppress his right to free speech for some other reason. Suppose the suppression was only incidental. Suppose the government had other, vitally important interests that needed protecting. And suppose that the resulting suppression of First Amendment freedoms was no greater than was essential to further those interests. Then the flag-desecration statute under which Johnson was arrested might pass the O'Brien test and be upheld.

Texas offered the justices two state interests that it sought to protect with the statute: preventing breaches of the peace and preserving the flag as a symbol of nationhood and national unity.

Referring to the first interest, the majority of justices agreed that "Texas claims that its interest in preventing breaches of the peace justifies Johnson's conviction for flag desecration. However, no disturbance of the peace actually occurred or threatened to occur because of Johnson's burning of the flag."

In other words, the Court said no harm, no foul. Referring to the second interest, the majority opinion declared:

> The State, apparently, is concerned that such conduct will lead people to believe either that the flag does not stand for nationhood and national unity, but instead reflects other, less positive concepts, or that the concepts reflected in the flag do not in fact exist, that is, that we do not enjoy unity as a Nation. These concerns blossom only when a person's treatment of the flag communicates some message,

and thus are related "to the suppression of free expression" within the meaning of *O'Brien*.

In other words, while Johnson's flag burning may have in some way damaged people's faith in their nation, that damage could only have been done by Johnson's message, which the state may not suppress, since it is protected by the First Amendment. In short, the Texas state statute failed the O'Brien test.

PUNISHING DISAGREEMENT
The majority opinion also dealt with the attempt by the government to regulate how individual citizens should view a national symbol such as the flag:

> We never before have held that the Government may ensure that a symbol be used to express only one view of that symbol or its referents. Indeed, in *Schacht* v. *United States*, we invalidated a federal statute permitting an actor portraying a member of one of our armed forces to "wear the uniform of that armed force if the portrayal does not tend to discredit that armed force." This proviso, we held, "which leaves Americans free to praise the war in Vietnam but can send persons like Schacht to prison for opposing it, cannot survive in a country which has the First Amendment."

That is, just as Schacht could not be punished for wearing an armed forces uniform while criticizing the nation's armed forces, Johnson could not be punished for burning a flag as a way of criticizing U.S. government policies.

The majority opinion also made a firm connection between freedom and dissent:

If there is a bedrock principle underlying the First Amendment, it is that the government may not prohibit the expression of an idea simply because society finds the idea itself offensive or disagreeable. . . . We can imagine no more appropriate response to burning a flag than waving one's own, no better way to counter a flag burner's message than by saluting the flag that burns. . . . We do not consecrate the flag by punishing its desecration, for in doing so we dilute the freedom that this cherished emblem represents.

In other words, one of the freedoms for which the flag stands is freedom of speech. Therefore, punishing people for desecrating the flag denies the very freedom for which the flag stands.

THE REHNQUIST DISSENT

There were four dissenting justices and two dissenting opinions. Justice John Paul Stevens wrote one of them. Chief Justice Rehnquist wrote the other, with Justices White and O'Connor also signing it. Rehnquist's lengthy (nearly five thousand words) and emotional dissent included quotations from "The Star-Spangled Banner" and the patriotic writings of Ralph Waldo Emerson and poet John Greenleaf Whittier.

The focus of much of Rehnquist's dissent was the flag itself, as in this passage:

The American flag, then, throughout more than 200 years of our history, has come to be the visible symbol embodying our Nation. It does not represent the views of any particular political party, and it does not represent any particular political philosophy. The flag is not simply another "idea" or "point of view" competing for recognition in the marketplace of ideas. Millions and millions of Americans regard it with an almost mystical reverence regardless of what sort of social, political, or philosophical beliefs they may have. I cannot agree that the First Amendment invalidates the Act of Congress [the Flag Protection Act of 1968], and the laws of 48 of the 50 States, which make criminal the public burning of the flag.

As for Rehnquist's opinion of the act of flag burning, his impassioned dissent equated it with murder: "Surely one of the high purposes of a democratic society is to legislate against conduct that is regarded as evil and profoundly offensive to the majority of people—whether it be murder, embezzlement, pollution, or flag burning."

As for flag burning as a form of expressive speech, Rehnquist argued that it was "no essential part of any exposition of ideas" but rather "the equivalent of an inarticulate grunt or roar that, it seems fair to say, is most likely to be indulged in not to express any particular idea, but to antagonize others."

QUALIFICATIONS TO THE RULING
In the majority opinion the Court was careful to note that its ruling did not make all flag burning legal in all instances. When a statute clearly attempted to limit the flag burner's free expression and so failed the O'Brien test, as the Texas statute had, then that statute would be declared unconstitutional.

The majority opinion left open the prospect that a state could prosecute flag desecration in two instances. First, if the act of burning the flag was likely to stir up an immediate violent response on the part of onlookers, then the flag burner might be prosecuted for creating a clear and present danger. "We do not suggest that the First Amendment forbids a State to prevent imminent lawless action," the opinion stated.

Second, an anti-flag-burning statute might be constitutionally applied if the statute was speech-neutral, and if the offending act was simple vandalism. The statute, therefore, would only be constitutional if it made no mention of expressive conduct and if no expressive content was involved in the flag burning itself. These qualifications would encourage opponents of the ruling to push for a new kind of law to protect the flag that would meet these qualifications. That law would be the Flag Protection Law of 1989, which would lead to the *Eichman* case.

eight
Aftermath

Reactions to the *Texas* v. *Johnson* ruling
were as varied and impassioned as the thinking of the justices who took part in its making. On the liberal side
Arthur J. Kropp, president of People for the American
Way, a liberal lobbying group, said the ruling was "a vic-
tory for freedom of speech." He added, "As a nation, we
are strong enough to withstand the pain of seeing our flag
burned. What we could not withstand is seeing the First
Amendment cast aside out of a misguided sense of
nationalism."

On the conservative side H. F. Gierke, the national
commander of the American Legion, said that he felt
"extreme sadness" at the ruling: "Many a Gold Star mother
[mothers who have lost a child in war] cherishes that carefully folded, triangular bundle of red, white and blue as the
closest link to a fallen hero son," he said.

William F. Kunstler, from the Center for Constitutional Rights, had argued the case for Johnson. He reacted
to the ruling by saying that it "forbids the state from
making the American flag a religious icon."

Kunstler would argue the case for the *Eichman* flag
burners as well. In his argument he would return to this
point: that although the flag may be sacred to some, to
burn the flag was not to commit a sinful and unholy act.

WILLIAM KUNSTLER (SECOND FROM LEFT) DISCUSSES THE SUPREME COURT
RULING TO DECLARE THE FLAG PROTECTION ACT OF 1989 UNCONSTITUTIONAL.
KUNSTLER AND DAVID COLE (SECOND FROM RIGHT) REPRESENTED SHAWN
EICHMAN (RIGHT), A DEFENDANT IN THE CASE, AND JOEY JOHNSON, A DEFEN-
DANT IN A SIMILAR CASE IN 1989.

INTERPRETING THE RULING

Don Edwards, a California Democrat, was a member of the
U.S. House of Representatives from 1963 to 1995. While
Texas v. *Johnson* was unfolding, he helped various individ-
uals and groups submit *amicus curiae* briefs in the case.

Edwards lent his help to people who supported
Johnson. After the *Johnson* decision, Edwards actively
opposed a new federal law that would make it a crime to
harm the flag physically. Edwards testified before the

Emergency Committee on the Supreme Court Flag Burning Case. As part of his testimony he sought to clear up misunderstandings about the *Johnson* ruling itself and about Supreme Court rulings in general.

MISTAKEN BELIEFS

During his testimony Edwards dealt specifically with three mistaken beliefs:

> Most of those seeking to reverse the decision, whether by statutory or Constitutional means, base their proposals on the mistaken belief that, in this case, (1) the Supreme Court overturned Mr. Johnson's conviction, (2) the Court extended the protection of the First Amendment to flag burning, and (3) the issue before the Court was whether flag burning was or was not symbolic speech. All these beliefs are false.

As for the first point, he said, "The essence of the Supreme Court's decision was to uphold the decision of the Texas Court of Criminal Appeals, which had already overturned Mr. Johnson's conviction." Here Edwards was addressing a common misconception about U.S. Supreme Court rulings: that they somehow "decide" a lower court case. The Court cannot decide a case that comes to it on appeal from the lower courts. All it can do is uphold or deny the lower court's ruling. If it denies the trial court ruling, the case goes back to that court, and authorities may decide to start from scratch and try the case all over again.

In this instance the Court affirmed the Texas Court of Criminal Appeals's decision. It was actually that state appeals court, not the U.S. Supreme Court, that over-turned Johnson's conviction. The U.S. Supreme Court simply affirmed that appeals court ruling.

DON EDWARDS, A CALIFORNIA DEMOCRAT, LENT HIS SUPPORT TO THE PEOPLE WHO WERE ON JOHNSON'S SIDE IN *TEXAS V. JOHNSON.*

Edwards also pointed out the misconception that the U.S. Supreme Court had let a guilty man off the hook:

Had the Supreme Court not heard Texas' case, Mr. Johnson would have been free (after jailing, trial, four years in court, thousands of dollars of expenses, and thousands of hours of his, his lawyers' and his supporters' time) more than a year ago. By taking the case, the Supreme Court did not "let off" a man who would otherwise have been imprisoned; rather, they subjected an innocent man to an additional year of costly legal punishment.

As for the second point—that the First Amendment now protected flag burning—that too was a mistaken belief. As a result of the *Texas* v. *Johnson* ruling, existing anti-flag burning laws across the nation had become unconstitutional. But the Supreme Court had stopped short of ruling flat out that any future flag-desecration law would be, by its very nature, a violation of free speech and therefore unconstitutional.

THE MEANING OF FLAG BURNING

What about the third point, the issue of whether flag burning was symbolic speech? No such issue was at stake in *Texas* v. *Johnson*. The majority opinion made that clear: "The expressive, overtly political nature of this conduct [Johnson's flag burning] was both intentional and overwhelmingly apparent."

As part of his testimony Edwards posed an interesting question: "What particular ideas might be expressed by burning a flag?" Here are some of his answers:

It might be opposition to idolatry in general, to the concept of the sacredness of physical objects. It might be opposition to particular actions carried out under that flag, whether by the government or by its agents (such as its soldiers). It might be opposition to governments in general, or to the particular government represented by the particular flag. It might be opposition to the government as being the legitimate representative of the people, or as acting in their interests or those of

others. One might express opposition to particular actions of the nation. One might express
opposition to the actions of the nation in general,
or to all people who support the government and
the flag.

Edwards then quoted from the Brennan opinion:
"Johnson was not, we add, prosecuted for the expression
of just any idea; he was prosecuted for the expression of
dissatisfaction with the policies of the country."

REACTIONS
Edwards then testified about dissatisfaction and flag
burning in reaction to the *Texas* v. *Johnson* ruling:

It is just such dissatisfaction that has motivated the
wave of flag burnings since the Supreme Court's
decision. Flags have been burned, for example, at
a gay and lesbian commemoration of the 20th
anniversary of Stonewall, at Puerto Rican nation-
alist rallies, by victims of American racism, and at
demonstrations for abortion rights. Flag burnings
have been reported in Boston, Austin, Albany,
Cleveland, Minneapolis, Portland, New York, Iowa
City, Berkeley, Little Rock, Rochester, San Francisco, Chicago, and Los Angeles.

These incidents helped fan the flames of outrage in
Congress that led to passage of the Flag Protection Act
(FPA) of 1989, which in turn set off more flag burnings,
including the incidents in Seattle, Washington, and Washington, D.C., in October 1989. Those incidents resulted in
the arrests and convictions of the flag burners whose
cases, when they reached the U.S. Supreme Court on
appeal, became known as *United States* v. *Eichman.*

nine
The *Eichman* Briefs

THE PETITIONER, OR APPELLANT, in *United States* v. *Eichman*—the U.S. government—filed petitions for appeal, asking the Court to reconsider and reverse the lower court rulings against two sets of respondents, or appellees. Though there were multiple respondents, in Court documents they are always referred to in the singular, as "the appellee" or "the respondent." The *Eichman* respondents were tried in Washington, D.C.

The other respondents were tried in Seattle, Washington. That case was known as *United States* v. *Haggerty*, named after Mark John Haggerty, one of the four Seattle defendants. Since the *Eichman* and *Haggerty* cases were so similar, the Court rolled them into a single case, named *United States* v. *Eichman*.

Supreme Court appeals are argued by lawyers for the two sides, who appear before the nine justices. Before the oral argument the lawyers submit written briefs that explain the case for each side.

The brief for the petitioner is written first. It tells why the lower court ruling should be reversed. It also lays the foundation for the oral argument to come.

Copies of the petitioner's brief are sent to the Court and to the respondent. A lawyer for the respondent then writes a brief in response. Copies of the respondent's brief are sent to the nine justices and to the petitioner.

U.S. Solicitor General Kenneth Starr argued the government's case in *United States* v. *Eichman.*

That way all parties have both briefs in advance of the oral argument.

THE Lawyers

The lawyer for the petitioner was Kenneth Starr. As U.S. solicitor general it was his job to argue the government's side in cases that went before the Supreme Court. Legal professionals consider being chosen for the office of U.S. solicitor general to be a great honor, as it is one of the highest offices a U.S. lawyer can attain.

Starr's background had prepared him for the office. He had served as a U.S. Court of Appeals judge and as a clerk to former Supreme Court Chief Justice Warren Burger. Starr would serve as solicitor general from 1989 to 1993. During that time he would argue twenty-five cases before the Court.

The lawyer for the respondent was civil rights attorney and activist William Kunstler. Unlike Starr he was a colorful man with a colorful background. Kunstler referred to himself as a "terrible kid," a gang member who committed acts of theft and petty vandalism. But during his school years he straightened himself out. He became an A student and went on to Yale University and then Columbia Law School. During World War II Kunstler served in the U.S. Army. He attained the rank of major and received the Bronze Star.

As a self-described radical lawyer, Kunstler had defended clients both famous and notorious, mainly in cases related to the First Amendment. His clients included the Reverend Martin Luther King, Malcolm X, and American Indian Movement (AIM) leaders. Later on in his career Kunstler would also defend Muslim terrorists.

THE PETITIONER'S ARGUMENT

To set the stage, each lawyer began his argument with a framing question. For the petitioner that question was

"Whether the First Amendment prohibits the United States from prosecuting appellees for knowingly burning a flag of the United States, in violation of . . . the Flag Protection Act of 1989. . . ."

Starr's question emphasized the First Amendment. That would be the thrust of his argument: to show how the First Amendment was not an obstacle to prohibiting flag burning. After the framing question, Starr presented his argument point by point.

PETITIONER'S POINT: NOT ALL SPEECH IS PROTECTED

Starr's opening point concerned the First Amendment:

> The United States does not dispute that appellees' flag burning constitutes expressive conduct. . . . But this does not doom Congress's considered judgment in passing [the FPA]. The First Amendment does not prohibit Congress . . . from removing the American flag as a prop available to those who seek to express their own views by destroying it.

Starr was right: the First Amendment did not mention the U.S. flag at all, so there could possibly be situations where using the flag in a political protest might be classified as criminal. But what about the conflicting issue of expressive conduct?

> This Court has never assumed that all speech, including expressive conduct, is entitled to full First Amendment protection. . . . The Court's decisions show that the protections of the First Amendment do not apply where . . . whatever value the expression may have to the speaker (or others) is

outweighed by its demonstrable destructive effect on society as a whole . . . and the speaker has suitable alternative means to express . . . whatever protected expression may be part of the intended message.

In other words, free speech has limits and may be suppressed if the speaker's words or actions are harmful enough to the welfare of others. Starr then cited precedent to back up this point about free speech limitations. He cited past U.S. Supreme Court cases in which the Court had affirmed lower court rulings limiting free speech.

One case Starr cited was *Chaplinsky* v. *New Hampshire*, with its "fighting words" limitation. He quoted from that opinion about categories of expression that "are of such slight social value as a step to truth that any benefit that may be derived from them is clearly outweighed by the social interest in order and morality."

Petitioner's Point: Flag Burning Should Be Added to These Exceptions Because It Disturbs the Peace Without Expressing Any Important Ideas

Starr quoted from Chief Justice Rehnquist's dissent in *Texas* v. *Johnson*, in which the Chief Justice compared Johnson's flag burning with Chaplinsky's fighting words, stating that "it may equally well be said that the public burning of the American flag by Johnson was no essential part of any exposition of ideas, and at the same time it had a tendency to incite a breach of the peace."

And so, Starr wrote, "For these reasons, the Court should treat the conduct at issue—physical destruction of a flag of the United States—as it has such other narrowly defined categories of expressive conduct that have not merited full protection under the First Amendment."

PETITIONER'S POINT: FLAG BURNING SHOULD BE PROHIBITED BECAUSE IT IS AN ASSAULT ON A CHERISHED SYMBOL

Starr had argued that flag burning was liable to incite breaches of the peace. Now he argued that it was dangerous in other ways. For one thing, he argued in the brief, the "physical destruction of the American flag, the unique symbol of the Nation, constitutes a violent assault on the shared values that bind our national community."

Starr then elaborated on what he meant by "a violent assault" on "shared values":

> [F]lag burning (or other forms of destruction or mutilation) is a physical, violent assault on the most deeply shared experiences of the American people, including the sacrifices of our fellow citizens in defense of the Nation and the preservation of liberty. . . . The flag stands as the most profound reminder that a physical assault on the Nation's unique symbol of community amounts, in the minds of the members of the community (and their elected representatives), to an assault on the memory of those who have sacrificed for the national community. . . . It is the physical assault and the accompanying violation of the flag's physical integrity . . . that occasion the injury that society should not be called upon to bear.

For Starr the flag was such a powerful symbol of all that the United States held dear that physically attacking it was a profoundly hurtful emotional experience for those who witnessed the attack. Here Starr was plainly taking the position that by physically assaulting the flag, the respondents were not just attacking a red, white, and blue piece of cloth. They were expressing contempt for all that the flag symbolized.

PETITIONER'S POINT: THIS CASE IS NOT A FIRST AMENDMENT ISSUE; THE FPA OF 1989 DOES NOT VIOLATE FREEDOM OF SPEECH

The 1989 amendment to the FPA eliminated the expressive language of "knowingly (casting) contempt upon the flag" from the original 1968 law. And so, Starr wrote, "[T]he amended statute focuses exclusively on the conduct of the actor, irrespective of any expressive message he or she might be intending to convey."

The 1989 FPA "fully ensures that only unprotected expression will be prosecuted," Starr wrote. "There is, thus, no danger that any individual would be prosecuted under the statute for what the person says about the flag." Therefore, "When viewed from the proper constitutional perspective, the Flag Protection Act fully comports [agrees] with the First Amendment."

Starr was now in a difficult, contradictory position. In the previous point he argued that those who attacked the physical flag also attacked everything that the flag symbolized, and that this was their real crime: injury caused by their symbolic expression of contempt. Yet now Starr was claiming that, under the FPA, the attacker was prosecuted only for attacking the physical flag—a mere piece of red, white, and blue cloth—and not for the real crime of attacking all that it stood for.

PETITIONER'S POINT: OTHER BRANCHES OF GOVERNMENT SUPPORT THE FPA

Starr's brief moved on to cite what he saw as overwhelming support for the government's side. He quoted support from the Senate Judiciary Committee: "The flag has stood as the unique and unalloyed symbol of the Nation for more than 200 years. In seeking to protect its physical integrity, Congress is simply ratifying the unique status conferred upon the flag by virtue of its historic function as the emblem of this Nation."

He also quoted from the House Judiciary Committee: "[The prohibition against flag burning] recognizes the diverse and deeply held feelings of the vast majority of citizens for the flag, and reflects the government's power to honor those sentiments through the protection of a venerated object."

And so, Starr wrote, "Congress . . . and the President . . . have now spoken with one voice—the physical integrity of the flag of the United States, as the unique symbol of the Nation, merits protection not accorded other national emblems."

Starr then added another objective. Besides *Eichman*, the government was asking the Court to reverse one of its own decisions: "To the extent *Texas* v. *Johnson* accorded flag burning full First Amendment protection, that decision should [also] be reconsidered."

PETITIONER'S POINT: THE COURT SHOULD DEFER TO ELECTED BRANCHES OF GOVERNMENT

Finally, Starr's brief asked the nine justices, who are appointed and not elected, to step aside and yield to the judgment of members of Congress, the people's elected representatives. Starr wrote:

> [The Court] should, we believe, defer to the considered judgment of the elected branches on the question of how important it is to the Nation to protect the flag from physical attack and destruction. With all respect to the Court, that is a judgment that the elected branches are particularly well suited to make.

Based on these arguments, Starr asked that the Court reverse both the lower court rulings in *Eichman* and its own ruling in *Johnson*. That was the case for the petitioner. Next came the case for the respondent.

THE RESPONDENT'S ARGUMENT

While the framing question in Starr's brief emphasized the First Amendment, Kunstler's two-part framing question focused on the FPA:

> Whether the Flag Protection Act of 1989, as applied to the expressive burning of a flag in an overtly political demonstration, violates the First Amendment to the United States Constitution.

> Whether the Flag Protection Act of 1989 on its face [clearly; obviously] violates the First Amendment to the United States Constitution.

That is, Kunstler was arguing that the FPA violated the U.S. Constitution both specifically, in regard to criminally punishing the *Eichman* flag burners, and generally, as a statute that was inconsistent with the First Amendment. That would be the thrust of the respondent's argument: to point out to the justices how the amended Flag Protection Act of 1989 violated the First Amendment and so was unconstitutional.

LINKS WITH *JOHNSON*

Kunstler, who had argued the *Johnson* case before the Court for the respondents the year before, began his argument by linking this case back to *Johnson*:

> The United States seeks to do in [*United States v. Eichman*] precisely what this Court barred the

State of Texas from doing in *Johnson*: "criminally punish a person for burning a flag as a means of political protest." ... To permit the government to incarcerate individuals merely for expressing opposition to its most political symbol would have grave consequences for the meaning of freedom of expression. This Court should reaffirm the principles articulated so recently in *Johnson*, and affirm the district courts' judgments.

Thus Kunstler reminded the justices of the precedent they had established in the *Texas* v. *Johnson* ruling: that criminally punishing someone for burning a flag as a political protest violated the First Amendment.

THE D.C. RESPONDENTS

Kunstler's brief then introduced the respondents, using declarations they had submitted to explain the actions for which they had been prosecuted. He first discussed those charged in the Washington, D.C., incident:

David Blalock, a veteran of the Vietnam War, explains that his service in Vietnam led him to associate the flag with United States intervention abroad, and that he burned the flag in opposition to such intervention.

Shawn Eichman, a New York artist, burned the flag to protest the United States' oppression of women and exploitation abroad.

Scott Tyler, a.k.a. "Dread Scott," a Chicago-based "revolutionary artist," burned the flag in part to protest the United States' oppression of Black people, and in part as a response to reactions to his art exhibit, "What is the Proper Way to Display a U.S. Flag?" Mr. Tyler's art exhibit caused a political uproar when it was displayed at the School of the Art Institute of Chicago in February 1989, and eventually caused Congress to add the clause in the current Act criminalizing "maintain[ing the flag] on the floor or ground."

Gregory Lee Johnson, of *Texas* v. *Johnson*, also took part in the Washington, D.C., flag burning. But authorities chose not to charge him with violating the FPA, so Johnson was not among the respondents.

To sum up, Kunstler wrote:

Defendants consider flag burning an essential element of their political expression, because for them, the flag represents not glory but oppression. Mr. Blalock, for example, states that "burning the Flag is a vital and indispensable means by which to communicate [his] message," because it is "a dramatic and total rejection of forced patriotism and the corruption that it conceals," and is "clearly understood by all the world's people."

Notice here how Kunstler took pains to pound home two key points: that each of the flag burners intended for his or her actions to convey a specific message, and that those messages were clearly articulated so that everyone could understand them.

THE SEATTLE RESPONDENTS
Kunstler's brief went on to make the same points about the actions of the Seattle flag burners. Carlos Garza was a Mexican American who burned the flag "to express [his] outrage over the mistreatment of Hispanic Americans by our government."

Jennifer Campbell was a University of Washington student who burned a flag "to strip off this blindfold of unquestioning allegiance and to cause people to focus on the suffering of people, both at home and abroad, and to thereby move America closer towards everything it is supposed to be."

Mark Haggerty burned a flag because "[t]he U.S. flag stands not for the people of the U.S. but for the power of the superrich ruling class as expressed through their government."

The fourth Seattle respondent, Darius Strong, wanted to "communicat[e] the idea that a person's freedom to express an opinion critical of the Government is of greater legal and moral value in America than the Government's authority to criminalize acts constituting demonstrations of . . . individual beliefs."

THE FPA

Kunstler's brief then moved on to the FPA of 1989, calling it "Congress's attempt to continue to criminalize flag burning and other specified flag conduct in the wake of *Texas* v. *Johnson*." Once Congress realized that the ruling made the existing FPA of 1968 unconstitutional, Kunstler wrote, it "sought to amend the flag statute to ensure that flag burning would remain a criminal act."

How did the 1989 amendment do this? "Congress removed the requirements that the actor 'knowingly cast contempt' by a 'public' act. It modified 'defiling' to 'physically defil[ing],' and added a proscription against 'maintain[ing the flag] on the floor or ground.'"

In other words, the 1989 Amendment removed all reference to what was protected by the First Amendment, the flag burner's symbolic expression. Now flag burning, unprotected by the right to freedom of speech, had been labeled a criminal act because it physically harmed the

WHAT IS THE PROPER WAY TO DISPLAY A U.S. FLAG?

In early 1989 *Eichman* respondent and artist Scott Tyler, who called himself "Dread Scott," created an art installation that was displayed at Chicago's School of the Art Institute. It became the center of a national controversy.

The work consisted of photographs of flag-draped coffins on a U.S. troop transport and South Korean students holding signs saying "Yankee go home son of a b---" and burning the U.S. flag. Photos were mounted on a wall along with a shelf of books with blank pages and a supply of ink pens. A U.S. flag was spread out on the floor below them. Viewers were invited to write their comments in the books. In order to do so they would have to step or stand upon the flag that was spread out on the floor.

Scott wrote, "When this work has been displayed, thousands of people filled hundreds of pages with responses. Many of those stood on the flag as they added their comments to the work."

Regarding the resulting controversy, Scott wrote, "President Bush Sr. declared *What is the Proper Way* . . . 'disgraceful' and the entire U.S. Congress denounced this work as they passed legislation to 'protect the flag.' Senator [Robert] Dole specifically noted that the law would apply to 'the so-called "artist" who has invited the trampling on the flag.'"

flag itself, not because it said bad things about what the flag stood for.

Now that Kunstler had introduced the respondents and presented their view of the FPA, he outlined his argument.

RESPONDENT'S POINT: DESECRATING THE FLAG DOES NOT HARM THE FLAG'S SYMBOLIC VALUE

Kunstler reached into U.S. history to link the respondents' actions with those of one of the Founding Fathers:

> The United States flag was born of a "desecration." When George Washington took command of the Continental Army at Cambridge, Massachusetts, in 1776, he defaced a British flag by ordering sewn upon it thirteen red and white stripes, subsequently referred to as "The Thirteen Rebellious Stripes." The question before this Court is whether the United States government may incarcerate its citizens for engaging in similar politically expressive flag desecration.

Kunstler was saying that the father of our country defaced a nation's flag to make an emotional political point of protest. If he could do that, then why couldn't the respondents in this case?

Kunstler's brief then made a point about what, physically, the flag amounts to: "[T]he flag is an infinitely reproducible symbol, and there is no showing that burning, temporarily defiling, or laying on the floor one or more of its representations harms its continuing function as a symbol."

That is to say, there is no such thing as "the flag," except as an abstract, symbolic idea. To harm a concrete, actual flag is not the same as harming that abstract, symbolic flag. They are two different things.

RESPONDENT'S POINT: THE FPA IS ACTUALLY DESIGNED TO PUNISH DISSENTERS

It was a long-held tradition to dispose of a worn-out or damaged flag by burning it. To address this tradition, a clause in the 1989 FPA read: "This subsection does not prohibit any conduct consisting of the disposal of a flag when it has become worn or soiled." Kunstler saw this clause as a discriminatory double standard:

> [T]he Act is not "aimed at protecting the physical integrity of the flag in all circumstances," for the same reason that this Court found that the Texas statute in *Johnson* was not so aimed: it contains an exception for the burning and physical destruction of worn or soiled flags. The Texas law is . . . designed instead to protect it only against impairments that would cause serious offense to others. . . . Thus, because a statute aimed at protecting the physical integrity of the flag in all circumstances is necessarily designed to suppress attacks on the flag's symbolic value, it would be unconstitutional."

In other words, according to the FPA, the flag could be lawfully burned, but only as a show of respect. Burning it as a show of disrespect was illegal. Therefore, the law discriminated against dissenters, denying them their First Amendment rights.

RESPONDENT'S POINT: PROHIBITING FLAG BURNING VIOLATES FREEDOM OF SPEECH

Kunstler again asked the Court to look back at its recent decision in *Texas* v. *Johnson*:

> In *Johnson*, this Court held that the government's interest in preserving the flag as a national symbol

is insufficiently compelling to justify a prosecution for political flag burning. While that interest allows the government to encourage people to respect the flag, it does not permit the government to compel people to show that respect under penalty of imprisonment. The same conclusion must be drawn here. The First Amendment was designed precisely to ensure that the majority not impose its notions of "consensus" on those who disagree.

Kunstler added another case as precedent that made the same point:

Johnson reaffirmed what this Court held forty-seven years ago in *West Virginia Board of Education* v. *Barnette*: the dual principles of freedom of expression and government by the people prohibit the State from mandating respect for its icons by imprisoning those who express disrespect. These principles compel dismissal of the prosecutions at issue here.

Thus Kunstler linked both the *Johnson* and *West Virginia* precedents with *Eichman*. All three cases, he was saying, involved punishing people for refusing to respect the U.S. flag. In both of the precedent cases the Court ruled that this punishment violated freedom of speech and so was constitutional. Kunstler was arguing that the Court should make the same ruling now.

Kunstler's brief also addressed the petitioner's point about the flag burners' behavior being offensive and their messages being unimportant and of slight social value:

The United States would have the Court rule that flag burning is unprotected expression because the government finds it an offensive and unimportant form of expression. But the First Amendment is needed precisely for expression that offends the government. The United States' proposed "exception" would swallow the rule of freedom of expression.

Again Kunstler's brief makes the point that the petitioner's case is based on punishing people who express disagreement with authority. By discriminating against dissent and dissenters, then, the FPA sets up two types of speech—agreeable and disagreeable—and labels the latter type criminal.

Attorneys William Kunstler (left) and David Cole met with reporters on the steps of the Supreme Court building after arguing against the Flag Protection Act of 1989.

ten
THE ORAL ARGUMENTS

THE NEXT STEP IS THE MOST DRAMATIC and decisive part of a U.S. Supreme Court case: the oral arguments. The justices have the briefs in hand with the arguments carefully outlined point by point. But briefs raise questions. The lawyers who wrote them must be there in Court, face to face, to give the justices the answers they need to make an informed decision.

The U.S. Supreme Court building is located at One First Street NE, across from the U.S. Capitol. It was built not just to house the Court but to symbolize the national ideal of equal justice for all.

At the back of the courtroom, where the arguments take place, is the bench where the justices sit, up on a platform backed by red velvet curtains. Court begins promptly at 10:00 a.m., when the clerk, the court official who calls out announcements, smashes down the gavel. Everyone rises, and the crier calls out, "The Honorable, the Chief Justice and the Associate Justices of the Supreme Court of the United States. Oyez! Oyez! Oyez!"

The curtains part, and the nine justices walk in and take their places at the bench. "All persons having business before the Honorable, the Supreme Court of the United States, are admonished to draw near and give their attention, for the Court is now sitting," the crier continues. "God save the United States and this Honorable Court!"

THE PETITIONER'S FOUR REASONS

The lawyers for each side, petitioner first, stand before the bench and face the justices. By tradition they do not read from their briefs or from any other sort of prepared text. Instead they speak extemporaneously to the Court until a justice interrupts with a question or comment. Each side is allowed half an hour for argument.

The oral arguments for *United States* v. *Eichman* took place on May 14, 1990. Solicitor General Starr began by addressing the framing question in his brief for the government: whether the Flag Protection Act of 1989 was constitutional.

"In our view," he said, "there are four reasons that argue powerfully in support of the constitutionality of this statute. First . . . Congress amended the Federal statute in response to *Texas* against *Johnson* to eliminate the prior, clearly content-laden language . . . 'cast contempt upon' and 'publicly.'"

He went on to the other three reasons: that the FPA does not prohibit people from dissenting through other means, such as speaking or writing; that burning the flag is such an abstract and general act that it does not express any concrete, particular ideas; and that flag burning is an assault on a cherished national symbol.

A CHALLENGE

Starr then moved on to focus on the facts and the nature of flag burning. The flag burners had handed out leaflets that expressed their concerns in words, but what if someone watching the demonstration had not seen one of these leaflets? Starr said:

> Now a passerby happening on these acts of flag burning would, in our judgment, likely and reasonably conclude that the actor is in a state of profound

disagreement. But it does not tell us with what. That message, the what, comes, if at all, from the speech that is incident or tied to the conduct as occurred in Street against New York. And that speech, of course, is fully protected, no matter how offensive that speech may be to the majority.

At this point a justice interrupted Starr. The transcript of the oral argument labels an interrupting justice as, simply, QUESTION. It is the nature of Supreme Court oral argument that justices interrupt to make a comment, ask for clarification, or directly challenge the lawyer's line of reasoning. In this case it was a direct challenge:

QUESTION: General Starr, I don't understand this line of argument. Is—is it that you're saying that somehow the expression "I hate the United States" is entitled to less constitutional protection than "I disagree with our policy in Eastern Europe"? Is that the point that—that if it's a political expression, it's too generic, too generalized, it's not entitled to the same degree of protection?

MR. STARR: The message itself enjoys the same protection. The question is what message is being conveyed. If one reads the statement—

QUESTION: Well, what you convey by burning the flag is, "I hate the United States."

In his answer, below, Starr responded aggressively. But notice the first four words of his reply. By tradition, the justices are to be treated at all times with deference and respect.

MR. STARR: With all due respect, that is not what is set forth in any of the statements in this record. . . . [W]ith respect to Carlos Garza, his concern . . . was with the treatment afforded Hispanic Americans. Not a word about hating the United States.

QUESTION: By reason of which he felt so strongly about it that it moved him to—to have feelings of animosity towards the country. What else does burning—surely burning the flag conveys something. What do you think it conveys if it does not convey the notion that, for whatever particular reason it may be, "I am in opposition to this country"?

Why was Starr having trouble here? He was trying to hold his ground and avoid conceding that the physical act of flag burning expressed a clear, definite message. To admit that it did would hurt his case, making it hard for the justices to accept the government's claim that the FPA of 1989 punished only a physical act and not an expressive act of speech.

Things turned difficult again later on, when a justice caught Starr in an apparent contradiction:

QUESTION: [W]ould you be concerned if in Eastern Europe or some foreign country a government punished demonstrators for marching with a defaced flag in support of the demonstrators' cause for freedom? . . . [I]sn't the point that this is a recognized—internationally recognized form of protest?

MR. STARR: We don't deny the fact that these individuals were engaged in a protest. What we are saying is the message of the burning of the flag itself is extremely limited.

QUESTION: Your original argument was that it was so general, so all-encompassing that it was not worthy of protection. Now you're saying that it's very narrow. I [am] not sure which it is.

Once again Starr was struggling. He could not seem to separate the physical act of burning the U.S. flag, which the FPA could punish, from the expressive message that lay behind the burning, which the FPA could not punish because it was protected by the First Amendment. Starr tried again to restate the government's position in a way that the justices would accept:

MR. STARR: One cannot punish a flag protester because he or she is expressing outrage about policies to the country. . . . [But] Congress does and should have power to protect the physical integrity of the flag as long as it is not saying we single out certain viewpoints for disfavored treatment. . . .

QUESTION: But in fact there is only one viewpoint: that you do not mutilate, deface, defile or trample upon the flag in order to show your love for the country.

Starr had done his best to convince a majority of the justices that, through the FPA, it was constitutional for the government to criminally punish the flag burners for harming the physical flag regardless of their expressive reasons for burning it.

THE RESPONDENTS' REASONS
Now it was the respondents' turn. Kunstler began by referring to his framing question: "We pose the question somewhat differently than was posed by the government. We think the question before the Court is, Can the government criminally prohibit flag burning, a form of political expression deeply critical of the government and anathema [detested by; accursed] to its officials?"

He moved on to three main points in the respondents' argument to come. The first was that *Texas* v. *Johnson* served as strong precedent in this case. The second was that the FPA of 1989 did not pass the O'Brien test, that its true intent was to suppress messages of disrespect or political dissent, which made it unconstitutional. The third was that there was no reason to accept the government's invitation to overturn *Texas* v. *Johnson*.

Next he returned to the FPA: "[The government] can do many things to persuade people to respect [the flag], to fly it, to indicate how it should be flown, to indicate the dimensions, to indicate the type of flag it should be and how it should appear, . . . but they cannot do it in a penal way [a way that serves as punishment]."

Kunstler referred to the FPA as a "direct attempt to get around *Texas* v. *Johnson*. . . . [I]t is not content neutral. It is content and viewpoint base[d]."

By saying it was "not content neutral," Kunstler meant that the FPA was not, as claimed by Starr, unconcerned with what was on the minds of the people who burned the flag. After all, the FPA expressly allowed the flag to be burned as a sign of respect, while singling out for punishment people who burned it as a sign of dissent.

CITING PRECEDENT

Kunstler then turned to precedent to support his comments on the FPA, referring to *Tinker* v. *Des Moines*, *Stromberg* v. *California*, and *Spence* v. *Washington*. First, he turned to *Tinker* to show how the Court had ruled against the singling out of another political symbol, black armbands:

> The record shows the students in some of the schools wore buttons relating to national political campaigns. . . . The order prohibiting the wearing of armbands did not extend to these. Instead, a particular symbol, black armbands worn to exhibit opposition to this Nation's involvement in Vietnam,

were singled out for prohibition. Clearly, the prohibition of expression of one particular opinion is not constitutionally permissible.

Then Kunstler quoted from the majority opinion in *Tinker*: "So it is a content-based statute. It singles out one particular political symbol, just as in *Stromberg* the red flag was singled out as one particular political symbol."

Finally he cited Chief Justice Rehnquist's dissenting opinion in *Spence* v. *Washington*: "Rehnquist said . . . it is the character not the cloth of the flag which the state seeks to protect. And I think that is essentially the truth of [the Flag Protection Act]. . . ."

In other words, the FPA was not really aimed at protecting the physical flag. Its real purpose was to keep the flag from being used as a tool of political dissent.

More precedent

At one point in the argument a justice interrupted and had Kunstler return to precedent:

QUESTION: Let's—let's—let's try fighting words, Mr. Kunstler. You know *Texas* v. *Johnson* was a year ago, and fighting words is no good why? I mean . . . it's certainly the case that whenever somebody tramples a flag or burns a flag there is a real potential for causing a riot, isn't there?

MR. KUNSTLER: Well, that isn't really what fighting words are as I understand *Chaplinsky*.

QUESTION: Well . . . it's the same thesis, that you don't have any rights to engage in conduct that's likely to provoke a riot.

MR. KUNSTLER: It really isn't, Justice—[flag

burning] isn't really fighting words. Fighting words, as I understand it, is what the Jehovah's Witness did in *Chaplinsky* when he went up to the sheriff and directly to him said words which would lead to a fist fight between two individuals. But much of speech provokes listeners, this Court has said many times, but maybe the highest purpose of speech is to provoke that kind of reaction. . . . I think *Terminiello* indicates how far you can go. At one point they were even throwing things.

Kunstler was right. The justice who mentioned "fighting words" was really referring to the "clear and present danger" test—not that the flag burner was trying to provoke a fistfight, but that the act of burning a flag might start a riot.

Kunstler went on to discuss "clear and present danger." He pointed out that "there has to be something that is . . . so probable that you're going to have bloodshed here, you're going to have a riot, and that doesn't exist here at all."

He closed by returning once more to the precedent of *Texas* v. *Johnson*:

> I would just like to close with the fact that . . . respect for the flag must be voluntary. We can understand people's enormous feeling for it. I think that's not difficult to understand. But it must be voluntary, and once people are compelled to respect a political symbol, then they are no longer free and their respect for the flag is quite meaningless.

> To criminalize flag burning is to deny what the First Amendment stands for, just what was said in *Texas* v. *Johnson*: "We do not consecrate the flag by punishing its desecration, for in doing so we dilute the freedom that this cherished symbol represents."

eleven
THE RULING

On the day that a ruling is handed down, the nine justices follow a time-honored routine. The associate justices' robes are kept in a changing room behind the courtroom. The chief justice joins them there, already robed, as they slip into theirs. Then they all shake hands and line up in single file behind the chief justice in order of seniority, waiting for the red velvet curtains to part. Then an aide sweeps them back, and the nine justices step in.

This was the same courtroom where the oral arguments took place a month earlier. On June 11, 1990, the ruling in *United States* v. *Eichman* would be delivered from the bench by its principal author, Justice William Brennan Jr., who also authored the *Johnson* ruling.

Reconsidering *Johnson*
The ruling was similar to that in the *Johnson* decision. The Court found in favor of the respondents by a 5 to 4 vote, with all nine justices voting the same way they did in *Johnson*. Conservatives Scalia and Kennedy joined liberals Marshall, Blackmun, and Brennan, while liberal Stevens sided with dissenters O'Connor, Rehnquist, and White.

The Court turned down the government's invitation to reconsider *Johnson* in order to align with the other two branches of government:

We decline the Government's invitation to reassess this conclusion in light of Congress' recent recognition of a purported "national consensus" favoring a prohibition on flag burning. . . . Even assuming such a consensus exists, any suggestion that the Government's interest in suppressing speech becomes more weighty as popular opposition to that speech grows is foreign to the First Amendment. . . .

The Court also rejected the government's contention that flag burning, like obscenity or fighting words, does not enjoy the full protection of the First Amendment:

[Respondents'] prosecution for burning a flag . . . is inconsistent with the First Amendment. The Government concedes, as it must, that [respondents'] flag burning constituted expressive conduct, and this Court declines to reconsider its rejection in *Johnson* of the claim that flag burning as a mode of expression does not enjoy the First Amendment's full protection. . . . Punishing desecration of the flag dilutes the very freedom that makes this emblem so revered, and worth revering.

THE FPA and THE O'Brien TEST

And how did the justices see the Flag Protection Act? Was it, like the Texas statute in *Johnson*, unconstitutional? The majority opinion conceded an important government point about the FPA: "It is true that this Act, unlike the Texas law, contains no explicit content-based limitation on the scope of prohibited conduct."

But then came the majority justices' judgment:

Nevertheless, it is clear that the Government's asserted interest in protecting the "physical integrity" of a privately owned flag in order to preserve the flag's status as a symbol of the Nation and certain national ideals is related to the suppression, and concerned with the content, of free expression. The mere destruction or disfigurement of a symbol's physical manifestation does not diminish or otherwise affect the symbol itself.

In other words, the FPA was, in fact, designed to suppress free expression. The burning of a physical flag did not harm the flag's value as a national symbol.

To explain the reasoning behind the judgment, the Court turned to the O'Brien test. The government's interest in protecting the flag for the sake of national unity did not pass the test, the opinion said. It was neither an important nor a substantial interest. Rather, it was related to the suppression of free expression.

The FPA was not content-neutral because it discriminated in terms of expression. It permitted burning that was done with respect for the flag, but it allowed the government to prosecute someone who burned a flag with disrespectful ideas in mind. And the government could not ban the expression of ideas, no matter how offensive they might be. Thus burning a U.S. flag was symbolic expression protected by the First Amendment.

A FATAL CONTRADICTION

As in *Johnson* the dissenting opinions in *Eichman* were highly emotional, strongly held, and sometimes contradictory. In his dissent Justice John Paul Stevens declared that in his eyes the FPA did pass the O'Brien test because "[T]he Federal Government has a legitimate interest in protecting the symbolic value of the American flag. . . ."

Just what was this symbolic value that needed protecting? "To us," Justice Stevens wrote, "the flag is a

THe STATUTeS In QUeSTION

Here are the relevant sections of the three statutes the justices considered in arriving at their opinions in *United States* v. *Eichman*.

The Texas State Statute
(a) A person commits an offense if he intentionally or knowingly desecrates:
>   (1) a public monument;
>   (2) a place of worship or burial; or
>   (3) a state or national flag.

(b) For purposes of this section, "desecrate" means deface, damage, or otherwise physically mistreat in a way that the actor knows will seriously offend one or more persons likely to observe or discover his action. . . .

The 1968 Federal Flag Protection Act
"Whoever knowingly casts contempt upon any flag of the United States by publicly mutilating, defacing, defiling, burning, or trampling upon it shall be fined not more than $1,000 or imprisoned for not more than one year, or both."

The 1989 Federal Flag Protection Act
(1) Whoever knowingly mutilates, defaces, physically defiles, burns, maintains on the floor or ground, or tramples upon any flag of the United States shall be fined under this title or imprisoned for not more than one year, or both.

(2) This subsection does not prohibit any conduct consisting of the disposal of a flag when it has become worn or soiled. . . .

reminder both that the struggle for liberty and equality is unceasing, and that our obligation of tolerance and respect for all of our fellow citizens encompasses those who disagree with us—indeed, even those whose ideas are disagreeable or offensive."

Yet Justice Stevens went on to write that "[T]he Government may—indeed it should—protect the value of the flag without regard to the specific content of the flag burners' speech." In other words, although the U.S. flag stood for the obligation to respect disagreeable ideas, that same flag had to be protected from people who would express those disagreeable ideas by desecrating it. This fatal contradiction stood at the core of the government's case. It could not be argued away.

THE FLAG'S SYMBOLIC MEANING
Another contradiction lay in how Stevens felt about the five majority justices. Nowhere in the *Johnson* or *Eichman* opinions did any of them declare approval of flag burning. In fact, all nine justices universally deplored it. Yet Stevens wrote:

> The symbolic value of the American flag is not the same today as it was yesterday. Events during the last three decades have altered the country's image in the eyes of numerous Americans. . . . [I]t is apparent that some thoughtful persons believe that impact, far from depreciating the value of the symbol, will actually enhance its meaning. I most respectfully disagree. Indeed, what makes these cases particularly difficult for me is what I regard as the damage to the symbol that has already occurred as a result of this Court's decision to place its stamp of approval on the act of flag burning.

The dissenting opinions of Justice Stevens and the other three justices would serve as encouragement for further attempts to criminalize the act of burning the U.S. flag as an expression of political dissent. In the years to come many lawmakers and private citizens would continue to fight for federal laws designed to protect the U.S. flag.

TWELVE
THE FLAG-AMENDMENT
DEBATE

THE *JOHNSON* AND *EICHMAN* rulings discouraged all prospects of creating a federal antidesecration law that would not be ruled unconstitutional, so flag protection supporters turned to a different strategy. They threw their energies into amending the Constitution. Their goal was to get a constitutional amendment passed that would authorize Congress to institute a law prohibiting flag burning. That way the U.S. Supreme Court would be highly unlikely to declare such a law unconstitutional.

The proposed amendment became known as the flag-desecration, or flag-burning, amendment. The amendment was only seventeen words long. It read simply: "The Congress shall have power to prohibit the physical desecration of the flag of the United States." The amendment would cover other forms of flag desecration, not just flag burning.

PERSISTENT ATTEMPTS

While the *Johnson* and *Eichman* cases were being decided in the Supreme Court, the amendment was being debated in Congress. During the 1989–1990 congressional session the proposed flag-burning amendment took up more time in Congress than any other issue. U.S. representatives and senators spent more than one hundred hours debating it.

From 1990 through 2006 Congress made seven attempts to pass the amendment. Since 1994 the House has passed it several times, but it has never passed in the Senate. The closest Senate vote was in 2006, when the amendment fell short of approval by a single vote.

During those years and beyond, the debate over the flag-burning amendment has continued both inside and outside of Congress. On one side are people whose primary objective is protecting free speech. They include members of the American Civil Liberties Union (ACLU) and People for the American Way, national organizations dedicated to protecting First Amendment rights.

On the other side are those who wish to protect what they see as the nation's most cherished symbol. Included are members of the American Legion, a community-service organization made up of war veterans, and members of Congress from both political parties, such as Republican Senator John McCain and Democratic Representative John Murtha.

Each side has its own reasons and supporters. Some reasons are familiar from the *Johnson* and *Eichman* cases. First, let's look at the reasons in favor of the flag-burning amendment. As we'll see, the supporters of the amendment base their support mainly on shared cultural values and moral and ethical concerns rather than on legal and constitutional matters.

REASON IN FAVOR: THE AMENDMENT WOULD NOT OUTLAW FLAG BURNING

U.S. Senator Dianne Feinstein of California explained that the amendment itself would not prohibit flag burning. She spoke from the floor of the U.S. Senate:

> This amendment would, quite simply, enable the Congress . . . to set the protocols governing our flag

DEMOCRAT DIANNE FEINSTEIN OF CALIFORNIA SPOKE OUT IN FAVOR OF THE
AMENDMENT TO BAN FLAG BURNING.

and protecting it as it has been protected
throughout most of this Nation's history. . . . It is
content neutral. It does not ban desecration,
burning, defiling, or anything else. . . . The resolu-
tion—if passed by three-quarters of the 50 State
legislatures—would merely return to Congress its
historical power to prohibit the physical desecration of the flag.

Senator Feinstein's description of the amendment contained a basic contradiction. The amendment would be "content neutral" and would not punish burning or other forms of flag desecration, she wrote. Yet it would "prohibit the physical desecration of the flag." How that desecration could be prohibited and yet not punished is not explained.

REASON IN FAVOR: FLAG BURNING IS NOT SPEECH

The U.S. Supreme Court ruled that flag burning is a form of speech protected by the First Amendment. Several precedent cases, beginning with *Stromberg* v. *California*, support the acknowledged legal fact that actions are a form of speech protected by the First Amendment. Yet supporters of the flag-desecration amendment disagree. U.S. Representative John Murtha of Pennsylvania said:

> No one would disagree that free speech is indeed a cherished right and integral part of our Constitution that has kept this Nation strong and its citizens free from tyranny. Burning and destruction of the flag is not speech. It is an act. An act that inflicts insult—insult that strikes at the very core of who we are as Americans and why so many of us fought—and many died—for this Country.

Retired Major General Pat Brady, an official with the Citizens Flag Alliance, a coalition of organizations dedicated to persuading Congress to pass the amendment, wrote:

> We do not believe that the freedom to burn the American flag is a legacy of the freedoms bestowed upon us by Madison and Jefferson and Washington and the other architects of our Constitution. . . . [T]he problem is those who call flag burning

speech. That is a distortion of our sacred Constitution and must not be allowed. Burning the American flag is not speech.

Reason in Favor: The Flag Is a Cherished Symbol

U.S. Senator Dianne Feinstein said:

The colors were chosen at the Second Continental Congress in 1777. We all know them well: Red for heartiness and courage; white for purity and innocence; blue for vigilance, perseverance, and justice. Even the number of stripes has meaning—thirteen for thirteen colonies. . . . The American flag is our monument in cloth. The flag flying over our Capitol Building today, the flag flying over my home here and in San Francisco, each of these flags, separated by distance but not symbolic value, is its own monument to everything America represents. And it should be protected as such.

U.S. Representative Tom Bevell of Alabama said:

As a veteran, I feel particularly strong about this proposal. Many men and women throughout our Nation's history have sacrificed their lives so that we could enjoy the freedoms we now have. The flag is a symbol of this country and a tribute to those who have protected our nation through the years. To allow individuals to desecrate this symbol for petty purposes is to cheapen the country for which it stands. I find it extremely offensive that laws cannot be passed by States to prohibit this kind of behavior.

Similar arguments, it will be remembered, were advanced by the government in the *Eichman* case and were rejected in favor of preserving First Amendment free speech rights.

REASON IN FAVOR: FLAG BURNING IS EVIL
Retired Major General Pat Brady wrote:

> We are convinced that our laws should reflect our values. Where in the Constitution does it say that toleration for conduct that the majority sees as evil is necessary for our freedom? Toleration for evil will fill our society with evil. Even those who oppose a flag amendment profess to be offended by flag desecration. Why tolerate it? What possible connection does toleration of evil have to the Constitution and our freedom?

Donald Tetreault, an official with the American Legion, wrote, "I understand that Congress cannot mandate honesty, loyalty, ethics, morality, or patriotism, but surely Congress can legislate against what is dishonest, disloyal, unethical, immoral, and unpatriotic."

Why tolerate what offends us? Why not legislate against what we find unpatriotic? These questions were addressed in the *Eichman* argument and answered in the ruling. However offensive flag burning may be, the Constitution says that such offenses must be tolerated.

REASON IN FAVOR: OTHER EXCEPTIONS HAVE BEEN MADE
U.S. Representative Jack Murtha said:

> There are, in fact, words and acts that we as a free Nation have deemed to be outside the scope of the

First Amendment—they include words and acts that incite violence; slander; libel; and copyright infringement. Surely among these, which we have rightly determined diminish rather than reinforce our freedom, we can add the burning of our Flag—an act that strikes at the very core of our national being.

Reason in Favor: The American People, Not the U.S. Supreme Court, Should Decide

Richard D. Parker, a Harvard Law School professor, said:

Consistently, the overwhelming majority of Americans has supported flag protection. Consistently, lopsided majorities in Congress have supported it too. In 1989, the House of Representatives voted 371–43 and the Senate 91–9 in favor of legislation to protect the flag. Since that route was definitively blocked by a narrow vote on the Supreme Court in 1990, over two-thirds of the House and nearly two-thirds of the Senate have supported a constitutional amendment to correct the Court's mistake and, so, permit the majority to rule on this specific question. Up to 80% of the American people have consistently supported the amendment.

After the amendment failed to pass the Senate by a single vote in 2006, retired Major General Pat Brady of the Citizens Flag Alliance issued this statement:

Despite an overwhelming majority of Americans that want our flag protected, the U.S. Senate has ignored the people they represent. Some Senators claimed that there are more pressing matters to attend to; however, it is never the wrong time to do

the right thing. While we are disappointed that the
flag amendment did not pass in the Senate, the Citizens Flag Alliance, representing 147 organization[s] and over 20 million members, remains
committed to returning the right of the people to
protect our flag.

Now let's look at the reasons for opposing the amendment. Notice that this opposition is based mainly on legal
and constitutional matters.

REASON IN OPPOSITION: OUTLAWING FLAG BURNING ONLY ENCOURAGES IT

Flag-burning expert Warren S. Apel, who operates a Web
site opposing the flag-burning amendment, wrote:

> The main cause of flag burnings since the end of
> the Vietnam war has been protest over flag burning
> laws. Flag burners in general are not "Anti-
> American." The people who want to "protect the
> flag" have incited more flag burnings than anyone
> else. So. Keep the law the way it is. Now and then
> someone will burn a flag to protest a war, or a law,
> or something. We should be strong enough as a
> country to accept criticism and allow some people
> to offend us now and then.

REASON IN OPPOSITION: FLAG BURNING PRESENTS NO THREAT TO THE FLAG OR TO THE NATION FOR WHICH IT STANDS

Journalist and political expert Hendrik Hertzberg wrote,
"The flag is not a piece of cloth, any more than the Constitution is a piece of paper; and the flag's sacredness is not
damaged when a piece of cloth representing it is burned or
trampled or used as an autograph book, any more than the

Constitution can be damaged by the destruction of a printed copy."

During congressional debate on the flag-burning amendment, U.S. Senator Russell Feingold of Wisconsin said:

> [T]his amendment is offered in the absence of any evidence, any evidence at all, that the symbolic value of the flag has in any way been compromised in this great Nation. It has not. No evidence has been offered to show that the small handful of misguided individuals who may burn a flag each year have any effect whatsoever on this Nation's love of the flag or our Democratic way of life.

U.S. Senator Robert Byrd of West Virginia said, "In the final analysis, it is the Constitution—not the flag—that is the foundation and guarantor of the people's liberties."

Reason in opposition: a flag-burning amendment would be unamerican

U.S. Senator Russell Feingold said:

> America is different from most other countries, and even from most other democracies. In America, all ideologies are protected, even those that the majority thinks are evil.
> Why is this right? Because the First Amendment was drafted and interpreted by people who intimately understood cultural, religious, and political conflict, and who knew how calls for censorship could launch the most bitter of culture wars.
> Passage of this amendment would result in peaceful protesters being arrested for making

political statements, something that happens in China, Iraq, or the former Soviet Union. Not something that happens in America.

reason In oPPosITIon: a FLaG-BurnInG amenDmenT woulD DamaGe THe ConsTITuTIon

Hendrik Hertzberg wrote:

If the proposed amendment is adopted, it will be the first time that the First Amendment, which is the Constitution's crowning glory, has itself been amended—and to constrict it, not expand it. . . . [T]he Constitution can and would be damaged, to the nation's shame, by the addition of something as inimical to its spirit as the flag-desecration amendment.

U.S. Senator Bob Bennett of Utah said, "When my Senate career is over, I don't want the most important constitutional vote that I have cast to be one that weakens the First Amendment."

reason In oPPosITIon: a FLaG-BurnInG amenDmenT woulD lImIT Personal FreeDoms

U.S. Senator Daniel Inouye of Hawaii, winner of the Medal of Honor for his service in World War II, said, "This objectionable expression is obscene, it is painful, it is unpatriotic. But I believe Americans gave their lives in many wars to make certain all Americans have a right to express themselves, even those who harbor hateful thoughts."

In a newspaper article about the amendment and the Confederate flag, Professor Eugene Volokh of the UCLA School of Law wrote:

AMENDING THE CONSTITUTION

The U.S. Constitution first went into effect in 1789. Since then, more than ten thousand amendments to the Constitution have been proposed. Only twenty-seven have been ratified, or approved and put into effect.

The first ten, taken together, make up the Bill of Rights, which was ratified in 1791. The most recent, the twenty-seventh, regulates changes in the salaries of members of Congress. It was ratified in 1992.

The process of amending the U.S. Constitution is a long and difficult one. First, the amendment must be passed by a two-thirds majority of both the U.S. House of Representatives and the U.S. Senate. Then, within a period of seven years, a 75 percent majority of the state legislatures—thirty-eight of the fifty states—must pass the amendment.

All fifty state legislatures have passed resolutions endorsing the flag-desecration amendment. The resolutions do show a strong willingness on the part of the states to pass the amendment, but they are not binding. First, Congress must pass it.

Right now, when people—mostly blacks—are deeply offended by what they see as a symbol of racism and slavery, the legal system can powerfully tell them: "Yes, you must endure this speech that you find so offensive, but others must endure offensive speech, too. Many Americans hate flag burning as much as you hate the Confederate flag, but the Constitution says we all have to live with being offended: We must fight the speech we hate through argument, not through suppression."

A FINAL WORD

The debate on flag burning and the Constitution continues on both sides, for and against. For now, though, the final word goes to Justice John Paul Stevens. In his 1989 dissent in *Texas* v. *Johnson*, he wrote:

> The value of the flag as a symbol cannot be measured. Even so, I have no doubt that the interest in preserving that value for the future is both significant and legitimate. . . . [S]anctioning the public desecration of the flag will tarnish its value—both for those who cherish the ideas for which it waves and for those who desire to don the robes of martyrdom by burning it.

In 2006 Justice Stevens spoke to the Chicago Bar Association on the subject of the proposed flag-burning amendment. In the seven years since *Johnson*, he said, he had changed his mind about outlawing flag burning. In Justice Stevens's opinion, passing the proposed constitutional amendment would be unwise.

"Nobody burns flags anymore," he said. "What once was a courageous act of defiant expression is now perfectly lawful and therefore is not worth any special effort."

This did not mean that Stevens now regretted his dissents in *Johnson* and *Eichman*. He remained convinced that he had interpreted the Constitution correctly back then.

But times had changed. "If one were to burn a flag today," he said, "the act would convey a message of freedom that ours is a society that is strong enough to tolerate such acts by those whom we despise."

NOTES

Chapter 1

p. 10, par. 2, The Flag Burning Page. http://www.esquilax
.com/flag/protection.shtml

p. 11, par. 1, Brief for the United States in *United States* v.
Eichman. http://www.usdoj.gov/osg/briefs/1989/
sg890147.txt

p. 11, par. 3, *United States* v. *Eichman* brief.

p. 12, par. 1, "About CCR." Center for Constitutional
Rights. http://www.ccr-ny.org/v2/about/mission_
vision.asp

p. 13, par. 2, "Presidential Quotes from Richard M. Nixon
to George W. Bush." www.allhatnocattle.net/Poppa
BushQuotes.htm

Chapter 2

p. 18, par. 4, *Stromberg* v. *People of State of California*, 283
U.S. 359 (1931). http://www.law.cornell.edu/supct/
html/historics/USSC_CR_0283_0359_ZO.html

p. 20, par. 4; p. 22, pars. 1–4, *Tinker* v. *Des Moines School
District*, 393 U.S. 503 (1969). http://laws.findlaw.com/
us/393/503.html

p. 25, pars. 1–4, *Schacht* v. *United States*, 398 U.S. 58
(1970). http://www.vlex.us/caselaw/U-S-Supreme-
Court/Schacht-v-United-States-398-U-S-58-
1970/2100-20079349%2C01.html

Chapter 3
p. 28, pars. 1, 3, p. 30, par. 4, p. 32; pars. 2, 3; p. 33, par. 1, *United States* v. *O'Brien*, 391 U.S. 367 (1968). http://caselaw.lp.findlaw.com/scripts/printer_friendly.pl?page=us/391/367.html

Chapter 4
p. 36, pars. 4, 5, *Schenck* v. *U.S.*, 249 U.S. 47 (1919). http://caselaw.lp.findlaw.com/scripts/printer_friendly.pl?page=us/249/47.html

p. 37, par. 4; p. 38, par. 2, *Chaplinsky* v. *State of New Hampshire*, 315 U.S. 568 (1942). http://caselaw.lp.findlaw.com/scripts/printer_friendly.pl?page=us/315/568.html

p. 39, par. 2; p. 40, par. 1, *Terminiello* v. *Chicago*, 337 U.S. 1 (1949). http://caselaw.lp.findlaw.com/cgi-bin/getcase.pl?friend=nytimes& court=us&vol=337&invol=1

Chapter 5
p. 44, par. 2; p. 45, pars. 1–2, *Halter* v. *Nebraska*, 205 U.S. 34 (1907). http://www.esquilax.com/flag/halter.shtml

p. 46, par. 1; p. 47, pars. 1, 2, *Minersville School District* v. *Gobitis*, 310 U.S. 586 (1940). http://caselaw.lp.findlaw.com/scripts/printer_friendly.pl?page=us/310/586.html

p. 47, par. 4; p. 48, par. 2; p. 50, par. 1; p. 51, pars. 2, 3, *West Virginia State Board of Education* v. *Barnette*, 319 U.S. 624 (1943). http://www.law.cornell.edu/supct/html/historics/USSC_CR_0319_0624_ZS.html

p. 49, par. 6, Sielicki, Jim. "Robert G. Heft, Designer of America's Current National Flag." Usflag.org. http://www.usflag.org/flagdesigner.html

p. 51, par. 3, *Halter* v. *Nebraska*.

Chapter 6
p. 54, par. 1, "U.S. Code Collection." Cornell Law School.

http://www.law.cornell.edu/uscode/html/uscode18/usc
_sec_18_00000700----000-.html
p. 54, pars. 4, 5–p. 55, par. 1; p. 55, par. 3, 4; p. 56, par. 2,
Street v. *New York*, 394 U.S. 576 (1969). http://www.law.
cornell.edu/supct/html/historics/USSC_CR_0394_0576
_ZO.html
p. 57, pars. 1–3, p. 58, par. 1, p. 59, par. 4, *Smith* v. *Goguen*,
415 U.S. 566 (1974). http://caselaw.lp.findlaw.com/
scripts/printer_friendly.pl?page=us/415/566.html
p. 59, par. 3, Kerrey, Bob. "Our Flag and Our Freedom."
Washington Post. June 15, 2006, p. A27. http://www
.washingtonpost.com/wp-dyn/content/article/2006/
06/14/AR2006061402005.html
p. 60, par. 3; p. 61, pars. 1–3; p. 62, par. 2, *Spence* v.
Washington, 418 U.S. 405 (1974). http://supreme
.justia.com/us/418/405/case.html

Chapter 7
p. 65, par. 2, *Revolutionary Communist Youth Brigade.*
Discoverthenetworks.org: A Guide to the Political Left.
http://www.discoverthenetworks.org/groupProfile.asp
?grpid=6406
p. 66, pars. 1, 2; p. 74, pars. 1, 4–p. 75, pars. 1, 2; p. 76,
par. 1, *Texas* v. *Johnson*, 491 U.S. 397 (1989).
http://www.law.cornell.edu/supct/html/historics/USS
C_CR_0491_0397_ZS.html
p. 67, par. 2; p. 68, par. 1, Jan Crawford Greenburg.
Supreme Conflict: The Inside Story of the Struggle for Control of the United States Supreme Court. Penguin Press.
January 2007. http://www.abcnews.go.com/GMA/
print?id=2811426
p. 68, par. 4, "Antonin Scalia." Oyez.org.
http://www.oyez.org/justices/antonin_scalia/
p. 70, pars. 1, 3; p. 71, pars. 1–4; p. 72, pars. 1–4, *Texas* v.
Johnson, 491 U.S. 397 (1989).

p. 73, par. 1, *Texas v. Johnson*, 491 U.S. 397 (1989). J. Kennedy, Concurring Opinion. http://supct.law .cornell.edu/supct/html/historics/USSC_CR_0491_ 0397_ZC.html

p. 76, par. 4–p. 77, pars. 1–3, *Texas v. Johnson*, 491 U.S. 397 (1989). C.J. Rehnquist, Dissenting Opinion. http://www.law.cornell.edu/supct/html/historics/USSC_CR _0491_0397_ZS.html

Chapter 8

p. 79, pars. 1–3, Greenhouse, Linda. "Justices, 5–4, Back Protesters Right to Burn the Flag." *New York Times.* June 22, 1989, p. A1. http://128.91.58.209/Articles/ 19890622_TexasVJohnson_1.pdf

p. 81, pars. 2–3; p. 83, pars. 1, 3, 4–p. 84, pars. 1–3, "Emergency Committee on the Supreme Court Flag-burning Case, 26 July 1989." The Flag Burning Page. http://www.esquilax.com/flag/testimony.shtml

Chapter 9

p. 87, par. 4, "William M. Kunstler, 1919–1995." The Flag Burning Page. http://www.esquilax.com/flag/kunstler .html

p. 88 pars. 1, 3–p. 89, pars. 1, 3, 4, 5; p. 90, pars. 1–3; p. 91, pars. 1–2, p. 92, pars. 1–5, Brief for the United States, *United States v. Eichman.*

p. 97, pars. 3–4, Dread Scott. "What Is the Proper Way to Display a U.S. Flag?" http://dreadscott.home.mind spring.com/whatis.html

Chapter 10

p. 103, pars. 3, 4, "How the Court Works." The Supreme Court Historical Society. http://www.supremecourt history.org/03_how/subs_how/03_a07.html

p. 104, par. 3; p. 105, pars 1, 5; p. 106, pars. 2, 7; p. 107, pars. 3, 5; p. 108, pars. 2, 3; p. 109–110, "In the Supreme Court of the United States." Oyez.org. http://www.oyez.org/cases/1980-1989/1989/1989_89_1433/argument/

Chapter 11

p. 112, p. 113, p. 115, *United States* v. *Eichman*, 496 U.S. 310 (1990). http://supreme.justia.com/us/496/310/case.html

p. 114, par. 3, *Texas* v. *Johnson.*

p. 114, par. 4, U.S. Code Collection.

p. 114, par. 5, Brief for the United States, *United States* v. *Eichman.*

Chapter 12

p. 117, par. 2, Associated Press. "Senate Panel OKs Flag-Burning Amendment." July 20, 2004. http://www.firstamendmentcenter.org/news.aspx?id=13747

p. 118, par. 5–p. 119, par. 1, Feinstein, Dianne. "Statement of Senator Dianne Feinstein." *Congressional Record.* June 27, 2006. http://feinstein.senate.gov/06speeches/cr-flag-protect.htm

p. 120, par. 3, "Murtha Champions Flag Protection Amendment." News from Congressman Jack Murtha. www.house.gov/murtha/news/nw010717.htm

p. 120, par. 4–p. 121, par. 1, "Major General Patrick H. Brady, Testimony before the Constitution Subcommittee, May 7, 2003." Citizens Flag Alliance. http://www.legion.org/cfa/flag/history/congress/testimony_brady/

p. 121, par. 2, Feinstein.

p. 121, par. 3, Bevell, Tom. "The Symbol of Our Nation." March 21, 1995. http://www.esquilax.com/flag/bevill.shtml

p. 122, par. 2, "Major General Patrick H. Brady, Testimony before the Constitution Subcommittee, May 7, 2003."

p. 122, par. 3, "Statement of Donald J. Tetreault." Citizens Flag Alliance. March 10, 2004. http://www.cfa-inc .org/?section=issues&subsection=issues_testimonies& content=testimony_donald (Accessed 12 June 2007).

p. 123, par. 1, "Murtha Champions Flag Protection Amendment."

p. 123, par. 2, "Statement of Richard D. Parker." May 7, 2003. Citizens Flag Alliance. http://www.legion.org/ cfa/flag/history/congress/issues_test_parker/

p. 123, par. 3–p. 124, par. 1, Associated Press. "Flag-Protection Group Vows Continued Fight." June 28, 2006. First Amendment Center. http://www.first amendment center.org/news. aspx?id=17082

p. 124, par. 3, Warren Apel. "Editorial." The Flag Burning Page. http://www.esquilax.com/flag/index2.shtml

p. 124, par. 4–p. 125, par. 1, Hendrik Hertzberg. "For Which It Stands." New Yorker. July 3, 2006. http:// www.newyorker.com/printables/talk/060703ta_talk_ hertzberg

p. 125, par. 2, Russell Feingold. "Senate Debate on Flag Burning." December 8, 1995. The Flag Burning Page. http://www.esquilax.com/flag/feingold.shtml (Accessed 23 July 2007).

p. 125, par. 3, Nat Hentoff. "Don't Burn Constitution to Save Flag." May 30, 2006. First Amendment Center. http://www.firstamendmentcenter.org/commentary .aspx?id=16944

p. 125, par. 4–p. 126, par. 1, Feingold.

p. 126, par. 2, Hertzberg.

p. 126, par. 3, Associated Press. "Flag-Amendment Foe Introduces Alternative Bill." July 5, 2005. http://www .firstamendmentcenter.org/news.aspx?id=15514& printer-friendly=y

p. 126, par. 4, Carl Hulse and John Holusha. "Amendment on Flag Burning Fails by One Vote in Senate."
June 27, 2006. *New York Times*. http://www.nytimes
.com/2006/06/27/ washington/27cnd-flag.html?hp&
ex=1151467200&en= 3caeb149d9e60823&ei=5094&
partner=homepage
p. 127, par. 1, Eugene Volokh. "What's Wrong With the
Flagburning Amendment?" *Los Angeles Times*. July 8,
2001. http://www.law.ucla.edu/volokh/flag.htm
p. 128, par. 1, *Texas* v. *Johnson*, 491 U.S. 397 (1989), J.
Stevens, Dissenting Opinion. www.law.cornell.edu/
supct/html/historics/USSC_CR_0491_0397_ZD1.html
p. 128, par. 5, Mark Sherman. "Stevens: Flag Burning
Change Not Needed." *Washington Post*. December 6,
2006. http://www.washingtonpost.com/wp-dyn/
content/article/2006/12/06/AR2006120601221.html

All Internet addresses were available and accurate when
this book was sent to press.

FurTHer information

Further Reading
Jordan, Shirley. *American Flag*. Logan, IA: Perfection
  Learning, 2003.
Kowalski, Kathiann M. *Order in the Court: A Look at the
  Judicial Branch*. Minneapolis, MN: Lerner Publica-
  tions, 2004.
*The Oxford Companion to the Supreme Court of the United
  States*. New York: Oxford University Press, 1992.
Travis, Cathy. *Constitution Translated for Kids*. Austin, TX:
  Synergy Books, 2006.

Web Sites
These Web sites are especially good places to pick up information and ideas on the issues discussed in this book.

Citizens Flag Alliance
http://www.cfa-inc.org/
A site dedicated to protecting the U.S. flag and supporting
  a flag-burning amendment to the U.S. Constitution.
  Includes a "How You Can Help" section.

Findlaw.com
http://www.findlaw.com/casecode/supreme.html
Free, easy-to-search database of U.S. Supreme Court
  opinions dating back to 1893.

First Amendment Center
http://www.firstamendmentcenter.org/
All about the First Amendment, including special sections on freedom of speech and flag desecration.

The Flag Burning Page
http://www.esquilax.com/flag/
Dedicated to keeping Congress from passing laws that
would reduce First Amendment freedoms, such as the
flag-burning amendment. Includes a history of flag
burning.

Supreme Court of the United States
http://www.supremecourtus.gov
Official site of the nation's highest court, packed with
information on the history of the Court, how the Court
works, and its current cases.

The U.S. Constitution Online
http://www.usconstitution.net
This site, aimed at young people, gives an in-depth look
at the Constitution, the Bill of Rights, the Declaration
of Independence, and some state constitutions.

BIBLIOGraPHY

Books

Curtis, Michael. *The Constitution and the Flag: The Flag Burning Cases*. London: Routledge, 1993.

Goldstein, Robert Justin. *Flag Burning and Free Speech: The Case of* Texas *v.* Johnson. Lawrence: University Press of Kansas, 2000.

Greenburg, Jan Crawford. *Supreme Conflict: The Inside Story of the Struggle for Control of the United States Supreme Court*. New York: Penguin Press, 2007.

Schneider, Richard H. *Stars and Stripes Forever: The History, Stories, and Memories of Our American Flag*. New York: HarperCollins, 2003.

Eichman Ruling

http://supreme.justia.com/us/496/310/case.html

Related Cases

Brandenburg v. *Ohio*, 395 U.S. 444 (1969).
Chaplinsky v. *State of New Hampshire*, 315 U.S. 568 (1942).
Halter v. *Nebraska*, 205 U.S. 34 (1907).
Minersville School District v. *Gobitis*, 310 U.S. 586 (1940).
Schacht v. *United States*, 398 U.S. 58 (1970).
Schenck v. *United States*, 249 U.S. 47 (1919).
Smith v. *Goguen*, 415 U.S. 566 (1974).
Spence v. *Washington*, 418 U.S. 405 (1974).

Street v. *New York*, 394 U.S. 576 (1969).
Stromberg v. *People of State of California*, 283 U.S. 359 (1931).
Terminiello v. *Chicago*, 337 U.S. 1 (1949).
Texas v. *Johnson*, 491 U.S. 397 (1989).
Tinker v. *Des Moines School District*, 393 U.S. 503 (1969).
United States v. *O'Brien*, 391 U.S. 367 (1968).
West Virginia State Board of Education v. *Barnette*, 319 U.S. 624 (1943).

index

Page numbers in **boldface** are illustrations, tables, and charts.

ABOUT THE AUTHOR

RON FRIDELL has written for radio, television, newspapers, and textbooks. He has written books on social and political issues, such as terrorism and espionage, and scientific topics, such as DNA fingerprinting and global warming. His most recent books for Marshall Cavendish Benchmark are *Gideon v. Wainwright: The Right to Free Counsel* and *Miranda Law: The Right to Remain Silent* in the Supreme Court Milestones series. He taught English as a second language while a member of the Peace Corp in Bangkok, Thailand. He lives in Arizona with his wife Patricia and his dog, an Australian Shepherd named Madeline.